CECILY PATERSON

Love Tears & Autism

An Australian mother's journey from heartbreak to hope

Copyright © Cecily Paterson, 2018

All rights reserved. No part of this publication may be reproduced, stored or transmitted in any form or by any means, electronic, mechanical, photocopying, recording, scanning, or otherwise without written permission from the publisher. It is illegal to copy this book, post it to a website, or distribute it by any other means without permission.

Cecily Paterson has no responsibility for the persistence or accuracy of URLs for external or third-party Internet Websites referred to in this publication and does not guarantee that any content on such Websites is, or will remain, accurate or appropriate.

Designations used by companies to distinguish their products are often claimed as trademarks. All brand names and product names used in this book and on its cover are trade names, service marks, trademarks and registered trademarks of their respective owners. The publishers and the book are not associated with any product or vendor mentioned in this book. None of the companies referenced within the book have endorsed the book.

This Second Edition published in 2018 by Firewheel Books.

(First edition in 2012 by Ark House Books.)

Second edition

ISBN: 13: 978-0-9944975-8-1

This book was professionally typeset on Reedsy.
Find out more at reedsy.com

Contents

Introduction	v
Prologue: a life-changing prayer	vii
The best laid plans	1
Changes and answers	8
The early signs	13
In my humble opinion… Other people's responses	21
Diagnosis	23
In my humble opinion… labels	34
Doing what the doctor said	36
So what is ASD anyway?	41
Eggs and therapy	43
Holland, and why I didn't want to join the secret club	51
Welcome to Holland	57
Going all domestic	59
Diet and the bio-med approach	68
Up and down and round and round with RDI	69
What will life be like for ASD children when they grow up?	79
Sticking together through it all	81
In my humble opinion… how much can you cope with?	88
God, grant me patience. And hurry!	90
In my humble opinion… Why do we avoid people who are a little bit different?	98
Taming the meltdown triggers	100
Siblings, loyalty and rivalry	108

What's the future for siblings?	114
I'm still just so unhappy!	116
In my humble opinion… the 'admiration reaction'	123
Angry and bitter on the couch	125
Depression: it's pretty normal	134
Praying for healing	137
Dealing with the aftermath	144
In my humble opinion… meeting the needs	153
It'll take a miracle	156
So, what about love?	165
What's happened since I wrote this book?	168
My standard advice for parents with newly-diagnosed ASD children	175
Appendix: The Relationship Development Intervention program	177
Extra resources	183
Books	183
Websites	186
Acknowledgements	190
A personal request from the author	191
Connect with Cecily Paterson	192
Also by Cecily Paterson	193

Introduction

When my second son was three, he was diagnosed with a condition that now afflicts more than 1 in 59 children, and rising—Autism Spectrum Disorder.

To try to come to terms with this news which had devastated our family, I read almost every book on autism I could get my hands on. I cried with sadness through most of them, except for the technical ones, which made me cry in frustration.

I wanted to find a book that was personal, practical, realistic and not too technical. I wanted a book that would let me know that I was not alone, and that there was hope for my son. I also wanted a book that was spiritual, that explored the questions of difficulty and suffering in the context of God's love.

I didn't find the book I was looking for, so I wrote it.

Love, Tears & Autism is, primarily, my own story. It explores how I felt, what I did, what I thought and perhaps most importantly, what I learned.

Like most stories, it doesn't start at the obvious beginning. Much of what I have learned in all of this has come about by examining old memories, past experiences and former beliefs. So I begin the story with some context.

The middle section is the technical part. After the immediate emotional impact of getting a diagnosis, I went on a crusade to find something—anything—that would help my boy. It was all about finding solutions.

It was only after we found what we believed was the way

forward that I then could sit back and really process it all. This was probably the hardest time for me—the time where I needed to ask my big questions and feel my big feelings—and so my story takes a more emotional and spiritual turn.

Finally, the story comes to an end. And again, like most stories, the ending is not really the ending. Our journey with autism continues, but what I really want people to know is that change is possible and hope is there.

Your story, or the story of your friend or your family member who has autism or who is suffering in some way will, of course, be different from mine. But I hope that you will know these things: that you can be honest with God and yourself; that you are not alone; that there is always hope; and that God is still there.

* * *

It's amazing to me that enough time has passed to publish a second, revised edition of this book. Even though the book finishes at the end of chapter 19, when my son was six, our story has kept on going. To keep you updated, and to stay relevant, I've added more links and up to date resources, and have also included a summary of our lives in the years since the book was originally published.

With love and prayers,

Cecily Paterson

Prologue: a life-changing prayer

It is a perfect Sydney day. The bright blue sky matches my mood. The view of the Harbour and the heads are a beautiful backdrop as I rock the baby in his pram. Everything is working for me today. The old cobblestones outside the church door make a perfect, gentle, rhythmic bump, bump on the pram wheels, just right for sending a young one to sleep. I breathe the fresh air in deeply. It is relaxing and I feel good, even though I am once again spending half the service outside because of a child.

It has become normal for me to only participate in a little bit of the church service. I don't like it to be that way because my faith is so important to me and I love singing, worship and prayer. But also important to me are my children and I know that their babyhood is only a short season. I have become used to sitting in the back with the pram, taking little containers of snacks to dole out at appropriate times, finding quiet toys to play with and knowing when I need to make an exit outside to settle someone.

The day is so joyful and so alive that I can't help but begin to pray as I move the pram back and forth over the rise and fall of the ground. It is as if I am pulled to prayer. I need to say thank you to the God who created this masterpiece of a world around me, who painted the sky and who made the feeling of even just breathing so loose and free.

I pray in my head. It would be mildly embarrassing to speak out loud. I thank God for the day, for my children, for my husband and the fact that his Bible college course is nearly finished. I pray for guidance and wisdom for the future. I pray about my husband's future job and ministry, and I ask God to give me a ministry of my own that will be effective and immediate and have a huge impact on people's lives.

I've never been known for having small ambitions.

Not being terribly good at concentrating too long when I pray, my mind is beginning to wander. The idea of having an effective, immediate, huge ministry is rather appealing. Perhaps it could be a speaking ministry—or intercessory prayer (probably not, as my mind wanders too much)—or counselling—or…

Suddenly I hit on just the right thing. I pray very specifically to God.

"I would like to have a ministry in which I understand people's true needs and motivations very quickly and can get right to the basis of whatever problem they have. Now, *that* would be a ministry and a gift worth having because it would be so useful to you."

And then a very unusual thing happens to me.

I often pray to God, but I don't often hear back from him. I am not a person who can say with confidence, "God told me…" or "The Lord has put it on my heart…" But today, I hear a voice speak to me. It's a very simple voice, and it just asks one simple question.

It asks, "Why do you want it?"

I am challenged, found out and humbled in five simple words.

"Yes, alright," I reply wryly to the voice. "I guess the real reason I want that kind of ministry is because it makes me look cool and godly and impressive and therefore popular in a weird sort of way."

I think for a minute. The day is still beautiful, fresh and bright. The baby is still asleep. I decide to ask God one more question.

"So—what do *you* want me to ask for?"

And a second very unusual thing happens to me.

The voice answers my question with one more simple sentence.

"I want you to learn how to love."

"Ok, Lord. I'll ask you to teach me to love," I sigh.

God lost no time in answering my prayer. Soon after I prayed asking him to teach me how to love, my three year-old son was diagnosed with Autism Spectrum Disorder (ASD) and Attention Deficit Hyperactivity Disorder (ADHD). I found myself on the hardest and most challenging journey of my life.

Over the next five years it felt as if everything I had and was and felt was being chewed up and spat out. My assumptions, beliefs, habits and thoughts were turned upside down and inside out.

There were many times when it was so difficult that I felt like going to bed and never getting up. There were a small number of times when I felt I might hurt my child or myself. There were times of happiness and joy, of course, but it felt for the most part that they were weighed down by a constant burden of sadness.

Through the dark times, I held on to the fact that I knew what the purpose of all of this was for me. God was teaching me to love, even when I felt no love and even when I wondered if I had the energy to face the next half hour.

I am so grateful that God shared his specific purpose with me. I would never choose autism for myself or my child, but through it, he is teaching me to love.

1

The best laid plans

I declared to the world at the wise old age of 16 that I *might possibly* get married, but I would certainly never have children. Children were too messy, too needy and too hard to control. Besides which, I was going to have an extremely high-flying and impressive career. I was a high achiever with big plans for my life.

I married Andrew, a law student, when we were both 22. And at the age of 24, sitting on the couch one night, I felt a surge of hormones rush through me. From that moment, the career and the 'no-children' declaration were forgotten. I swapped one plan for another. I wanted babies and I wanted them now.

We drove a large, green family sedan, and when I sat in the front seat and looked behind me I could imagine a group of three little children sitting happily in the backseat. They were clean, washed and brushed. They had blonde curls and lovely manners. They were spaced two years apart, were all healthy and smart and came from easy pregnancies and happy births.

That was the plan. I assumed that having children and all that went with it was within my control. If I heard stories about infertility or miscarriages or children born with disabilities, I shut my eyes to them, shuddered and thought, 'how awful. But that happens to other people. There's no way I could cope with it if it happened to me, so I'm going to pretend it doesn't exist and make it all go away.'

But as I quickly found out, things were not going to happen according to my plans. In fact, my plans were given a big shake-up by God.

To begin with, it took me twelve months to fall pregnant the first time. Every month that went by with no result felt like an eternity. I felt desperate, emotional and worried. Would I ever have a baby? Both Andrew and I were ecstatic when the pregnancy test read positive.

I had an easy pregnancy, so I put the waiting behind me and concentrated on the baby. Our daughter, Jasmine, was born in 1999, a healthy girl as beautiful as a dove. We were besotted and so were the rest of our relatives. We moved into our new house in our new neighbourhood, joined a new church, settled down and began the task of raising our family.

Unfortunately, that 'family' wasn't arriving as per my schedule.

When Jasmine turned one, I thought we had probably better do something about trying for the second child because it had taken so long the first time. I abandoned my birth control regime and hoped for the best. Again, the months went by with no result.

This time, however, I had a friend in my efforts. Sarah was a young mum from church with a little boy a year older than Jasmine. We met up for regular play dates and sanity sessions on long hot afternoons. Our children enjoyed playing together and as time went on, we found ourselves sharing more and more of our lives.

"I'm really getting worried," I confided one afternoon as we listened to the children zooming their trains and cars up and down in the next room. "We've been trying to conceive another baby for eight months now and nothing seems to be happening."

"I've been trying for a year longer than that," she replied. "I don't really know what to do about it. I don't want to go down the IVF road. I don't even know if it's right to go and see a doctor about it. Maybe God only wants to give me one baby. But I really would like a bigger family."

"Why wouldn't God want you to have more than one child?" I said. "Even if you don't want to do IVF, there must be steps before that, surely? And it's not wrong to go to the doctor. You'd go if you had a broken leg wouldn't you?"

It was the beginning of a very interesting journey with very interesting results for both of us.

Sarah started first, seeing the local fertility specialist. I followed, a month after her. The diagnosis in both our cases was a failure to ovulate regularly. We both began to take tablets that would help. If they didn't produce a result within six months, we would go back and try something new.

The only things the tablets produced in my case were severe cramping pains for two days in the middle of every month. After six months of trying, but no pregnancy, both Sarah and I stopped taking them. It had now been 18 months for me of trying to conceive, with no baby in sight yet.

The next step was to have my tubes checked for blockages. This involved sitting straddle-legged and open under an x-ray machine while dye was pumped up into my fallopian tubes. We watched to see if the dye would go all the way through the tubes, or if there was a blockage somewhere. It was uncomfortable and embarrassing, but I tried to make light-hearted conversation with the radiologist.

"What's that white shape showing up in the x-ray?" I asked. It was moving across the screen and I didn't think it looked like any of my organs.

"Oh, that's just a fluff," she said, grinning.

"A fluff?" I asked, confused. "I've never heard of that. What's a fluff?"

"You know—gas," she explained, going a little bit pink in the face.

"Oh," I nodded, trying not to look as humiliated as I felt.

But for all the embarrassment, the test showed a result. My tubes were blocked. I was booked into hospital to have keyhole surgery. Once my tubes were cleared, if all went well, there would theoretically be no reason why Andrew and I couldn't have another baby.

A few months later, the surgery was done. I was clearly still ovulating, judging from the back-breaking pains every month, and it seemed that we could try again for our baby.

Finally, almost exactly two years after we had begun waiting for our second baby, I fell pregnant. Andrew and I were overjoyed. As we had done with our first pregnancy, we told the world from the very start. I felt suitably ill and tired, but we were both so excited that I didn't mind. I felt bad for Sarah, but she was gracious and generous and wished me all the best.

Week five, week six and week seven passed as normal, but in week eight something strange happened. For a few days I didn't really 'feel' pregnant any more. And then I started to bleed.

It was if a stone had been dropped into my stomach when I saw it. 'This can't be right', I thought. 'I'm not having a miscarriage. No. This is the baby we've been waiting for so long'.

I rang Andrew at work in a panic of tears.

"You've got to come right away. Something's happening to the baby."

I was so distraught that I didn't even get into my clothes

from the pyjamas I was still wearing and we turned up at the hospital casualty department with me in pink and blue flannelette. Andrew explained what was going on to the nurses while I sat numbly on the hard plastic seat, trying to keep my baby alive in my thoughts.

They ushered us in for an ultrasound and then a young doctor told us the bad news.

"I'm afraid it looks like you're going to lose the baby. We're not sure whether it is just a miscarriage or whether it is an ectopic pregnancy, so we'll take some blood tests and see what happens over time."

"What's an ectopic pregnancy?" I asked. I'd never heard of it.

"It's where the embryo gets stuck in the fallopian tube. It keeps growing, but because it's not in the womb it's not viable. If it grows too much, the tube can burst and then you can be in serious trouble with internal bleeding, so we would have to take it out. Plus, it can damage the tube."

This was bad news. It was hard enough to lose the baby. It was even worse to think that I might have a damaged fallopian tube, after all I had been through with them already. Surely that would mean it would be harder for me to be pregnant in the future?

I sat and cried for hours while they did tests and we waited. We waited all that day, and then we waited some more over the next few days. I had regular blood taken to test the levels of pregnancy hormones in my body, but I wasn't getting any clear answers.

"We're still not sure what's going on," the doctor told me a few days later. "Go home again, take it easy and you'll probably miscarry naturally in the next few days. But call me if you have any pain or if anything unusual happens."

We waited for a week. I felt ill and unwell and I was still bleeding. Finally, my mother persuaded me to go to our regular

GP. To be honest, I went only to keep my mother happy because I wasn't expecting much from him. He was a good doctor, but every time I had taken our daughter to him he said something like, "Don't worry, she will get better. If she's not better in three days, come back, but just let her get some rest." He was reluctant to give drugs, reluctant to order significant tests and generally happy to let viruses take their natural course.

I drove up with Jasmine and told him what had been going on. He sent me for an immediate ultrasound and told me to come straight back. When I arrived for the second time in his office, he said, "You've got an ectopic pregnancy. You have to go to hospital."

"Oh," I said. "So do I ring them up and go in tomorrow? How does this work?"

"No," he said. "You're going now. You probably shouldn't even be driving by yourself. Your tube could erupt at any moment and you could bleed to death. I'll ring and tell them what's going on, so go now."

Such strong words from my usually cool and collected GP were worth taking notice of. I drove home in a panic, found a babysitter for Jasmine, called Andrew home from work, and took myself straight to the hospital.

Andrew and I waited for eight hours for me to go into surgery. Finally, late at night, he went home to be with Jasmine. I stayed alone, looking at the ceiling and shivering slightly under the hospital blanket. At midnight, after hearing at least two groaning expectant mothers being wheeled past for caesarean sections, I was finally taken into theatre.

We lost our baby and I lost my left tube. Rather than having keyhole surgery, I was cut open because the internal bleeding was getting so bad. Recovery took six weeks, in which time I cried and cried. I cried for the baby that died, I cried because I was scared of not conceiving in the future, and I cried because I wanted a baby so much.

We planted a tree in our garden for the sweet soul that we had nurtured for just those few weeks. I felt better, seeing new life growing, but the new life I really wanted to see was a baby inside my womb, and I wasn't sure it was ever going to happen.

2

Changes and answers

It was October 2002 and Sarah was on my mind in a big way. She had now been trying to conceive for more than three years and was facing some fairly intensive fertility treatment. I couldn't imagine trying for a baby for another whole year with no success, so I put my ectopic pregnancy aside and decided to hold a prayer meeting for her.

Over the past several years, I had seen many answers to my prayers and I was beginning to embrace the idea of working out what I wanted and then praying very specifically about it. Lots of Christians pray to cover all their bases, often in these terms: "Please God, could you do this, but if you don't want to, then help me to accept your answer. As long as it's your will, Lord…"

I decided that wasn't for me. Praying specifically is risky because you're putting yourself out there asking God to do something that he may or may not do. Praying in general terms seems safer. It's easier to cope with a 'no' answer if we pray that way, but then, I have never really liked 'safe'.

Sarah and her husband seemed ok with the idea of being the subjects of a prayer meeting, so we invited a number of good friends and asked them to pray specifically for more children for them.

We met in the crèche room after church one Sunday. It was an emotional time. More than half of us were crying by the end. We were making ourselves vulnerable, admitting our sadness for our friends and sharing their grief and frustration. Sarah and her husband stood in the centre of our circle while we put our hands on them and poured out our hearts to God. "Please, give them more children," I prayed. "You love children and you love these guys. They are great parents. They desperately want more children, and you can give them their hearts' desires. Please do it."

In my secret heart I added, "And please, give me another baby too. I, also, feel desperate and sad. Only you can do this."

The emotions faded, the excited expectation waned slightly and life went on. Both Sarah and I now found ourselves in the position of needing to pack up our houses and make a plethora of arrangements as we would both be moving out of the area at the end of the year. Sarah's husband had been offered a job in the north of the State and we were moving to Sydney so that my husband could start a four-year course at Bible college.

Apart from all my normal fears about moving ('Will I make friends? Will I cope? Will Jasmine be happy?') and my specific fears about Bible college ('Is being the wife of a minister something I really want to do?' and 'Will we manage without a regular income for four years?') I was also worried about my apparent infertility in a community where infants and toddlers just seem to appear from nowhere. Bible college students these days love to breed, and a lot of them have big families. I hoped that I would be able to manage my emotional state with the constant pop, pop, pop of new babies that I would almost certainly see around me.

But I didn't have to worry. In early December, I saw the double lines on the pregnancy test again. It was positive. I was pregnant.

And an early scan showed that the embryo had made it to the right place.

I rang Sarah, happy but tentative. How would she respond to my good news? Again, I didn't have to worry. She had news of her own.

"I'm pregnant too," she told me. It was an absolute joy. Our due dates were mere days apart. God had brought us so far together, and had answered our prayers. We felt that all the anguish was over. We didn't know at that stage that the journeys were really only beginning.

What Sarah's journey would require of her became apparent a few days later. She rang me one afternoon.

"I've just had a scan," she said, and waited. "It's not just one baby," she added, in a very understated way.

"Oh my goodness!" I practically screamed down the phone. "You're having twins."

"No," she said. "Not twins."

"What?" I gasped. "T-triplets?"

It was true. She was pregnant with triplets, and had enough morning sickness to prove it. It blew my mind every time I thought about it. How she was going to cope in a new town with three babies? Next time, I decided, I would pray specifically for one baby at a time. God had answered my prayers, but in over-abundance.

Secretly, I felt strange. Sarah was facing a big challenge and a massive change in her life. Her pregnancy was complicated. Her life to come would be even more so. My pregnancy by comparison was very simple, and I wrestled with a feeling of dismay at being ordinary.

In my most honest moments, I can admit to myself and to God that all my life I have wanted and worked to be special, to be different from others and to stand out. It motivated me to be the best and the smartest all through school and throughout my short career. I love success and applause, and I'm terrified of failure and criticism. Sometimes being successful is an overwhelming need and sometimes it's less obvious but it is always there, and it's not something I'm proud of. I usually try to hide it under layers of apparent humility and politeness, but I know my heart, and I know God knows it too.

I was so thankful to God for this pregnancy, but secretly I also wanted it to appear special to everyone else around me. Little did I realise that God would use the child that was to come to really teach me about being special and different and successful. I would be going on a journey where I would realise just what success and failure really mean. I would be learning about acceptance and love and where my worth really comes from.

But I pushed all that down and aside. Right now, the job at hand was moving. Moving house, moving church, moving job, moving city, moving friends and moving from having an income to living on government support.

My husband started as a full time student at Bible college, and the three of us, together with a bump that kept growing, moved to Sydney to begin a new chapter in our lives.

To help pay for college and cover our living expenses, my husband and I shared a part-time job at a small church. They provided us with a house to live in and a little bit of spending money. In return, Andrew worked a day and a half and I worked two days, running services, helping with Kids Clubs, teaching Scripture and leading Bible studies. It was busy, especially for Andrew. His study load turned out to be much heavier than we had expected, and with both of us living where we worked, it seemed that we never had any time to stop.

To make matters more stressful, the minister of the church announced a few months later that he would be leaving to take up another position. His date of departure was in the same week that my baby was due. The church took on a locum for a couple of days a week, but we felt the weight of responsibility fall heavily on us.

My pregnancy went smoothly, despite the work pressures. I had hardly been sick to begin with, and my second trimester was almost enjoyable. I was very happy to hear about the safe birth of all three triplets, only about four weeks premature. Sarah had done an incredible job. And then, in not too much time, finally, Cameron's due date came around.

After six hours of drip-induced labour, my baby boy was sucked into the world by a vacuum extractor at the hands of the on-duty hospital registrar. He was big, beautiful and healthy. I was content, and exhausted and tearful and joyous—all the things that new mothers are. God had answered my prayers and had given us a wonderful new baby.

3

The early signs

My dreams had come true. Not only did I have my baby, I had an easy baby! From the start, Cameron was extremely convenient to live with.

He was placid, easy to put to sleep and easy to entertain. The only problem I really had was his waking every three hours for more food until the age of about eight months. Because of all the milk he drank he was also the fattest baby I'd ever seen.

In the early months, he passed all his milestones with no problems. I thought he was gorgeous because he smiled a lot and slept during the day. I did occasionally notice that if we tried to get his attention to play with him, he would often look away or appear not to notice us. I didn't think about it much at the time and put it down to him perhaps being tired. I was never an overly anxious mother who saw disaster in every tiny cough and sniffle, and I believed in the 'he'll grow out of it' solution to most problems.

When Cameron was six months old, we took a trip up the coast. He enjoyed the travel and seemed to look around him, even if he was mostly interested in the motel's TV remote control. On our way to Queensland we called in for a day with Sarah and the triplets. Although I would never have said Cameron wasn't normal then, I was puzzled by the difference between him and his three new friends. The triplets were wriggly little things, investigating toys, trying to get around the room and intensely alert. By contrast Cameron looked a little like a beached whale—he just lay on his back and gurgled! I put it down to him being so chubby that he literally couldn't move like they could. Plus, there were three of them to entertain each other so of course they would be more alert.

There were no obvious signs of autistic spectrum disorder in the first year. Looking back I can see some signs that things were heading in that direction, but for the most part Cameron was a happy little chap and we were delighted to have him.

Things changed a little when Cameron turned one. He was starting to get grizzly and hard to get on with. On his first birthday he came out from his nap to find the room full of relatives and birthday cake. He wasn't happy and screamed solidly and at full volume for about half an hour. He only calmed down after we all made a deliberate effort not to look at him. (I later found out that this is often a child's first encounter with a day that is markedly different from normal. First birthday celebrations are an important milestone and families generally have a big celebrate to mark the occasion. If a child has ASD it can be totally overwhelming for them.)

As time went on, that became a bit of a habit: if he was the centre of attention, he tended to scream. He was happiest if people didn't talk to him and didn't look at him. He didn't seem to be able to handle it.

Just to make my life busier, I had begun designing and selling cuddly cute fitted cloth nappies. I needed a brochure to go with them, so one day I set up a makeshift photographic studio, decked Cameron out in his brightest nappy and set about taking some photos of my little model.

Where most babies would respond to their mother's face and voice and give happy smiles with enough coaxing, Cameron would not help me out. I took some great pictures of him side on and facing away from me, but I did not get a single face-on shot where he was looking straight at me. I felt annoyed, but not curious enough to do anything about it. More time would have to pass and a lot more questions would have to be raised before I started to join the dots and figure out what was going on inside his brain.

The second year of Cameron's life was when we started to notice more of what we called his eccentricities.

To begin with, he hardly felt any pain. I was proud of my tough little fella. Unlike his big sister who was always 'more sensitive' (which is a nice way of saying a complete sook), if Cameron fell over, he just got up and kept on going. Most other children would have been screaming with some of the knocks he took, but he hardly seemed to notice.

"He should be a football player," I said proudly. Little did I know that feeling no pain is a feature of an underdeveloped central nervous system and interrupted brain pathways. Even though it is not specific to autism, children with autism can suffer from it.

He also had an absolute obsession with pressing buttons. If we visited my parents, he would run straight through the door, ignoring his grandparents, and head for the switches on the video, TV, remotes, lights, phones, computer, fans, oven and any other gadget he could find.

For a long time I tried the tactics that had worked with Jasmine from the age of eight months. I would say "Cameron, no!" in a deep growl. I would remove his hand, take him away from the situation and try to distract him with something else.

It didn't work the first time, and it never ever worked after that. If he was removed happily, he'd head straight back for the switch and keep pressing. If he wasn't removed happily he would then proceed to throw an enormous tantrum for half an hour. Once he was done screaming, he would then head straight back to the switch and keep pressing.

After a lot of effort, I realised it was hopeless to even try, so I gave up worrying about the switches in our house. For a while I made a half-hearted effort in other people's places to show that I was a respectable mother, but most of the time I just moved things out of his reach as best I could or tried to ignore it.

Something that worried me more was the fact that he continued to look past people and avoid their gaze. In fact, he got very upset if most people looked at him, spoke to him or in any way acknowledged him. Again, I made efforts to get him to look at family and friends to say hello and goodbye, but after months of failure my efforts were mostly token and for show so that others wouldn't think I was a hopeless or irresponsible parent.

As time went by, I was starting to get more concerned about his speech. He just didn't talk. Not only that, he didn't seem to understand things either. Other children about the same age seemed to be able to 'get' concepts like 'Mummy's got a baby in her tummy', or 'we're going to the shops now' or 'this is a birthday party and we're having cake'. Cameron seemed oblivious to most things around him. He lived only for the immediate moment.

He also couldn't make transitions. Every day is made up of transitions from one activity to another. It had always been easy to explain to his sister at the same age, "First, we'll eat breakfast, then we'll go and get dressed. Now we can play outside and in five minutes we have to go inside…" But every transition made Cameron hysterical. Moving from one simple activity to another was distressing and difficult for him.

When I asked people about this, the advice they gave was to keep to a routine and do the same things every day.

"He'll get used to it. Maybe it's the novelty that he's not handling," they said.

But I had always stuck to a basic routine. It would be hard to accuse me of too much spontaneity in my life. And it still didn't answer the fact that he didn't seem to even understand what I was talking about.

Perhaps most dangerous was the fact that Cameron ran away. He ran away all the time, wherever we went, as far as he could go and extremely quickly. From being a baby who hardly moved, once he finally began to walk, he suddenly found some speed and my days of carrying on adult conversations in unfenced areas were over. We lost him onto main roads twice and spent two very long, very scary 15-minute periods searching for him when he disappeared on the Bible college property.

All of these things made me start asking questions. I just didn't feel right about his development. But at the same time there seemed to be lots of normal things too. He was affectionate with us. He adored his big sister and would play with her as much as he could. He seemed to eat well enough, although he was incredibly picky, and he was growing. He also didn't have frequent illnesses like some of my friends' children.

However, he was getting harder and harder to manage as he got older and bigger. I had felt myself to be a pretty competent parent of my now six year-old daughter, but I was at a loss as to what to do about Cameron's tantrums and his odd behaviour.

I talked a lot to my friends about him. By this time we had moved again and were now living on Bible college property along with 12 other families. Most of the women were stay-at-home mums like me with growing families, so we met daily around the swings and trampoline to watch our children play.

I was interested to watch and see what the other children of Cameron's age were doing in comparison to him and I would often say, "I'm a bit concerned. Look—he's not even close to doing what your child is doing."

Inevitably I would get one of two answers. Either, "Oh, he's a boy, and boys are different from girls," or, "He'll grow out of it. They're all different."

Although I tried to feel reassured, I knew that something more than just 'being a boy' was going on. By the time he was two and I was happily pregnant with baby number three, I was ready to get some help.

Somehow, I didn't connect all of his behaviours together as being part of the same problem. I knew about delayed speech, so that was easy to focus on as a 'real' problem. I rang the local health centre and booked in for some speech therapy. They had a look at him and said I should join the 'tiny talkers' program they had for children who weren't communicating well.

I turned up at the parents-only session with Cameron as I had been unable to find a babysitter. He was loud, restless and wriggly. I chased him down the halls, and tried to shush him in the room and bribe him with toys to play with, but we left early, after enough annoyed looks had been shot my way by other parents who clearly had been more successful in their babysitter recruitment. I did take home the literature, read it dutifully and tried to do everything they said, but nothing really seemed to improve.

I went to the GP a little later and stated my case—again focusing on his lack of speech.

"He doesn't seem to talk, except for saying 'no' all the time, and copying exactly what his sister says," I explained. "Do you think he could see a paediatrician?"

The GP knew about our lack of funds as Bible college students and wanted to save me some money. "I think the paediatrician would just refer you to a speech therapist so why don't we try some individual therapy first and cut out the middle man," he said.

I duly went to six sessions with a woman who tried some things and said that Cameron had lots of language but was not using it appropriately. In not so many words she also indicated that I wasn't tough enough with him and if I was stricter, he would get the hang of it. He did seem to improve a little from the therapy, but it was expensive and I was now heavily pregnant so we didn't continue going. I thought I could continue on with what she had shown me at home.

When the new baby, Max, was born, things really disintegrated. Cameron had meltdown after meltdown all day long for hours at a time. He would run away, crawl under the furniture, kick and scream and resist anything I tried to do. I have a very vivid memory of pulling him out from under the TV cabinet by the ankles because I was afraid he would hurt his head in his rage. I couldn't take him anywhere because he was uncontrollable. I didn't know if he would run away, burst into screams or just refuse to do whatever I asked him. I even resorted to buying a popular child discipline book and tried to implement some 'naughty spots' because I thought he was just a very difficult little boy.

But again, nothing worked. His behaviour did not improve. The meltdowns did not abate. He was angry, crying and frustrated for much of every day. If I wanted him to do something I had to carry him or fight him or just do it myself. I constantly carried smarties in my handbag so that I could bribe him to get in and out of the car, and even that didn't always work. I was beside myself with worry and fatigue from dealing with him, recovering from a caesarean section, caring for a new baby who also screamed for hours every day and solving the problem of a chronic cough that my six year old daughter brought home from school.

Life felt like it was falling apart at the seams and I felt like the one who was supposed to hold it all together, but I was failing dismally. If I could just find the right solution, everything would be fixed, surely?

The new year came and as Cameron approached the age of three, it was becoming more and more apparent that he was not just 'picking it up', as all my friends had assured me that he would. Things were not improving. I needed more answers.

My husband's parents had been caring for Cameron for a day each week during my pregnancy with Max. It had allowed me to do some work on my first book but it also gave my father-in-law, a retired GP, plenty of time to observe Cameron's behaviour. Three months from Cameron's third birthday, he said to me, "I think you should get this child to a developmental paediatrician. He's got some problems."

I felt relieved. Here, finally, was someone who could see what I had been talking about! I took his advice and headed straight for the GP.

In all my visits to the doctor before, I had been sweet, gentle and willing to do whatever they suggested. This time, my attitude was different. I knew what I wanted, and I was going to get it quickly. I marched in to the medical centre almost the next day and said, "All I want is a referral to a developmental paediatrician. Please write the letter for me." I got it on the spot and rang up for the appointment.

But any hopes for sorting out this problem speedily were quickly dashed. Unfortunately the next available appointment wasn't for another three months. I made it anyway, and settled down to wait. Surely soon I could get the issues ironed out and get my son on the right track. Surely the problem was going to be easily fixed.

In the three months of waiting, I found out what Cameron's problem really was. And to my utter shock, the person who told me was a preschool teacher, over the telephone.

* * *

In my humble opinion… Other people's responses

This is a conversation I had over and over again in the year or so before Cameron was diagnosed.

Me: "I'm a bit concerned about Cameron. He doesn't seem to be speaking much compared to his sister at the same age."

Friend: "Really? He's probably just a bit slower. All kids develop at their own pace. You know Einstein didn't speak until he was like, six or something. Anyway, he's a boy. Boys are always slower than girls."

Why did almost everyone give this response? I think there are a few reasons for it.

Perhaps they wanted to make me feel better. Perhaps they didn't want to acknowledge that any child might have something wrong with them because it feels uncomfortable and scary. Maybe they didn't have time or interest to get involved in my worry or maybe they felt they wouldn't know what to do if there really was a problem.

The first reason is the nicest, and I'm sure it was behind the vast majority of responses I got to my concerns. However, even though wanting to make people feel better comes out of kind intentions, it actually tries to shut out the person who is expressing the worries. For more than a year, I was really, really concerned about my boy, but I found hardly anyone willing to listen or to acknowledge that there might be a problem, so keen were they to make me feel better about it.

The other reasons are normal too. I know, to my shame, that I have avoided other people's problems in the past. I hope that I have a little more grace, patience and generosity now.

I have personally learned from this. If I hear a parent express worry about their child now, I ask questions about it.

"How long have you been worried about it? What do you think you might do about it? What would ease your mind about it?" I tell them about my own experience and I encourage them to take the child to a paediatrician who will listen to them and take them seriously.

4

Diagnosis

In the three months that we had to wait before we could see the paediatrician, I was watching Cameron carefully and writing down things I noticed.

One of his particular foibles was what we called his 'stuck' routine. It first appeared as we left his grandparents' house one Thursday. Without much convenient parking, I usually left the car on the street about 50 metres from their front door. It was always tricky getting Cameron inside the house, and getting him back into the car was another whole drama again. He either fought to stay in the house, refusing to go out or ran as fast as he could to the car with me panicking behind.

On this particular day he was in a running mood. He darted around the corner and headed right for the car. I breathed a sigh of relief as I saw him approach the door, and then yelped as he sped right past. I put on a burst of speed myself as I yelled frantically for him to stop. He ran another 20 metres before coming to a halt right next to the driveway to his grandparents back gate. Frustrated and angry, I grabbed his hand and yanked him back to the car. He yelled and screamed with all his might and we had a mega-tantrum for the next half hour while I drove home.

The next week, it happened again, but this time I was prepared. I caught him just five metres past the car, but he was not coming back to the car for anything. He pulled and urged forward with all his strength yelling and shrieking, "Stuck, stuck, stuck."

When his little hand finally slipped out of mine, he tore up to the same place next to the driveway that he had stopped at the previous week. "Stuck, stuck, stuck!" he tantrumed.

Once he had stood there for a couple of minutes, he calmed down and then was fine to come with me and get into the car.

When I finally understood autism, I realised that he was creating routines and habits that helped him maintain control. He needed to follow his own static rules in order to feel better about the world. For the next six months, every time we tried to leave his grandparents' place, he had to go through the routine of running up to his 'stuck' spot and standing there for a few minutes until he felt ready to get into the car.

The 'stuck' routine had a few variations. Every time we came home he wouldn't go inside the house unless he could stand next to the garage for a few minutes. Then he had to run to the end of the outside verandah, from where I had to coax (and usually carry) him through the front door, with him resisting all the way.

I developed a routine of my own in order to cope. I shooed Jasmine through the door first, then carried in Max in his baby capsule, unloaded whatever groceries or bags I had in the car, and then finally steeled myself for the inevitable fight to get Cameron in. The last step was always locking the front door behind me as I didn't want to have to do it all over again if he made an escape.

There were other odd behaviours that were becoming more obvious too. By this time his speech had improved so that we could actually understand what he was saying. But all he was saying were stories, scripts and lines from TV programs.

I remember being absolutely delighted but then completely flummoxed by the first real words that I ever heard from him. It was an almost complete rendition of the song 'Dorothy the Dinosaur' by the Wiggles.

His speech had certainly not improved enough for him to understand or answer questions. He was completely floored by any question, even something requiring only a yes or no answer. As for "What's your name?" or "How old are you?" or "What's your favourite toy?"— it was a waste of time to even ask it. He would just turn away or yell in protest.

Then of course, there was the picky eating. He would only eat pasta and cheese, vegemite sandwiches, yoghurt and apples. No meat, no vegetables and nothing with any colour in it. He refused food with strong smells, refused food that was on the wrong plate, refused food with the wrong number of items on the plate, and refused food, well, just because he did.

He was also picky about clothes. No jeans or jumpers, jackets or hats. No sweatshirts or t-shirts with designs on them. No button-up shirts or vests or ties. He refused to wear anything but track pants and long sleeved t-shirts in solid colours. He had his favourite shoes, and I hoped against hope that his feet wouldn't grow too fast, or that the shoes wouldn't wear out too quickly because I couldn't see how I would ever get him into anything else.

Then there was his inability to toilet train and his refusals to get into the bath. Night-time routines for my daughter had always been a fairly straightforward 'dinner, bath, teeth, story and bed'. Cameron fought his way through dinner, he refused, kicking and screaming, to have a bath and he clenched his jaw shut when I brought out the toothbrush. Thankfully he enjoyed the story part, but it often took him hours to get to sleep.

He was also addicted to music and TV. If I wanted to keep him calm, I would often put a children's show on. It worked for as long as the show lasted. Once I went to turn it off, however, the screaming started. He also needed to watch all the beginning and end credits, and seemed far more interested in the logos and slogans than in the shows themselves.

A bigger addiction was Thomas the Tank Engine which occupied his whole world for about three or four months that year. (It came back at various stages over the next three to four years.) He talked about Thomas constantly once he started to get more words. His first words on getting up and last words on going to bed were 'Thomas is a tank engine. He has six small wheels' or 'Gordon is number 5. Thomas is number 1. Henry is number 4'. I became a great, if somewhat reluctant, expert on Thomas and his annoyingly jovial group of engine friends.

I didn't realise at the time that Cameron hardly ever used his hands for pointing, gesturing, writing, holding, squishing, feeling or splashing. What I did notice was that he always had to hold two items in his hands. It might be two small books, two cards or two train engines. In his Thomas phase, he carried a yellow carriage and a blue carriage around in his hands all day every day for months. It was a monumental disaster one day when one went missing. He cried and cried for hours and we ended up buying a whole new set just to get the same colour carriage as a replacement.

There was also his **inability to make choices**. Many of our peers followed parenting philosophies that declared that giving children choices was not good for them. I didn't agree, and was more than happy to give my children the choice between, for example, the red t-shirt or the blue t-shirt, or juice or water, or an orange or an apple. In Cameron's case, I wondered if perhaps the no-choice people were right because as soon as he was presented with two things to choose between, he would scream loudly and run away.

I have a photo of all three children together at around the time Cameron was diagnosed. The fact that he was actually sitting in the frame with his brother and sister was quite amazing. For the entire year leading up to this point, it had been a major issue to get him to be in a photograph with anyone else. Surprisingly, he loved smiling for the camera on his own, but when he had to be part of a group, he would yell, run away and resist fiercely.

The photo shows up one of his typical features from this time—his glassy eyes. He rarely looked right at people, but kind of 'through' them. I have a vivid memory of looking back at him sitting in the car as he stared blankly at his trains, ignoring everyone around him. It made me feel almost sick with fear. It was as though he was sinking into his own little abstract world of unreality and we'd never be able to get him out.

I wrote much of this down in preparation for the appointment with the doctor. I didn't 'see' everything at that stage, and lots of these things are things I look back at now with a better understanding. Looking at it now I can't believe that I couldn't see how everything linked together and made a picture of a child with severe cognitive and social difficulties. But I didn't know about autism, and I would never have wanted to know about it. I didn't want to know about anything that wasn't completely in the range of 'normal' as I knew it, and I was not ready to admit that my child was anything but a little bit eccentric.

In fact, 'a little bit eccentric' were the exact words I used on the phone to the director of the preschool I was booking Cameron into for the following year.

In the midst of all of the worries about our son, my husband was in his final year of Bible college and had been looking for a job for some time. In June of that year, he secured an appointment as an assistant minister in a small, pretty town south of Sydney. As soon as we knew where we were going at the end of the calendar year, I found a preschool and rang to put Cameron's name down.

"I'd like to book my three year old in starting next February," I told the director. "But I think he's going to need some special care—he's a little bit eccentric."

Her ears immediately pricked up. "Eccentric? What does he do?" she asked.

"He yells a lot. His speech is delayed. He only really speaks in 'slogans' or scripts. He has a lot of trouble transitioning from activity to activity and he is obsessed with trains. He really only likes to play by himself," I said, laughing a little bit apologetically, trying to not make it sound as serious as it was. "He's seeing a paediatrician soon just to check there's nothing really wrong."

"I don't want to be rude," she said, "but I think he might have an autistic spectrum disorder."

I can still feel the flump of my stomach turning over as she said it. It was a complete shock. In one conversation my son had gone from being a 'bit eccentric' to having a serious diagnosable condition.

I could hardly tell my husband when he got home. Autism was a big, heavy word and I almost felt apologetic as I said it, as though I was just being a bit of a hysterical, over-worried mother.

He raised his eyebrows. "Really? I mean, he's not sitting in a corner banging his head against the wall."

For a few weeks I thought it wasn't true. I prayed that it wouldn't be true. When my husband was out at college I surreptitiously googled autism. I did it quietly because I didn't want to admit that I was taking it too seriously. I found a number of pages about autism with lots of difficult medical terminology. Some things seemed right, but not everything. I tried to let it go and not worry, but then I heard it again.

At church we were friends with a woman who had worked with a children's charity and who had a lot of experience with children in need. She took a liking to 'Cam', as she called him and after hearing me voice my worries about his speech a number of times, she took it on herself to observe him more closely. In the same week that she suggested 'autism', another friend, this one a child psychologist, said the same thing after watching him playing in a group of children for an hour or more.

In three weeks, I had three unofficial diagnoses—all for the same condition—autism.

I hit the computer and researched and read for hours. By about the sixth week, I was absolutely sure that we were waiting for a diagnosis of autistic spectrum disorder. And I was absolutely shattered.

Andrew and I were both nervous when we drove across Sydney for the visit to the paediatrician. It was a grey day, the traffic was heavy and Westmead, where we were headed, is an ugly, concreted suburb. We were snippy and short with each other, anticipating all the usual difficulties in keeping Cameron in check while we tried to talk to the doctor, and worrying about what the doctor might say.

I also had a small wrestle going on in my thoughts. At the same time that I was praying that he would say, "There's no problem. He'll be fine. Go away and don't fret," I was also a little concerned that Cameron wouldn't show his worst behaviour and the doctor wouldn't believe that there was anything wrong.

But I really needn't have worried.

As soon as we stepped into the waiting room, Cameron found

the trains in the toy box. He was happy for about five minutes. After a while he started looking for all the switches and buttons that he could press. Then he went through all the animals in the animal box.

Why are doctors always late? After a good half hour of waiting, Cameron was well and truly set to leave. Unfortunately, we hadn't done what we had come for yet. The nurse was ready, however. She wanted to take his measurements, so we wrestled him onto the scales for a routine weigh-in and tried to stretch him out to have his height checked. He began to yell, and really didn't stop after that.

The doctor, who seemed a quiet, serious sort of person, finally came out to see what the noise was and invited us in to his consulting room where he watched Cameron's anxiety and hyperactivity and autistic behaviours increase in frequency, pitch and volume. When he tried to talk to him or look at him closely, Cameron yelled and screamed and ran to the other side of the room. I was able to calm him for some of the time by holding him on my knee and singing, but it was clear that this was a child with some serious issues.

Amidst the noise and chaos, we told the doctor what we had observed and what we were worried about. He took a family history, a health background and copious notes, and finally after a nerve-fraying, noisy hour-long consultation, he asked me, "What do you think it might be?"

I said, "I think it's autism".

He replied, "I think you're right. He has autistic spectrum disorder. With some ADHD added in."

And that was that. At the age of three years and one month, Cameron had an official diagnosis.

I had another wrestle in my head. Half of me was devastated

about the outcome. 'Autistic' is a terrible word for any parent to hear about their child. But the other half of me was relieved. Finally, I knew what was going on.

If a problem has a name, you can find a solution to it. That has always been my attitude. In my own head, I am the solutions queen. A few years before, I had found a way to buy our ideal home when it was supposedly already sold. I had found a way to cure myself of a year of chronic pain in my hands that the doctors didn't know what to do with. I had found a way for us to live on no income for four years of Bible college. I had great faith in my ability, with God's help, to negotiate around any problem and I was very confident in the fact that I was here in the right place, talking to the expert who knew about these things, looking for solutions for my child's difficulties.

Unfortunately, there weren't any.

The paediatrician was a nice enough man. He knew his stuff, he made a good diagnosis and he wrote a helpful report. But I was expecting more.

My questions to him were, "So, what do we do now? What will the outcome be for Cameron? How can we help him? What's the treatment?"

His answers were vague at best. He couldn't promise any kind of outcome. There was no standard treatment. He talked a little about possibly using medication to some advantage when Cameron was older, but he was still too young for that.

He did say three definitive things. Firstly, we should contact the Autism Association. Secondly, we should see someone for speech therapy. And thirdly, we should make sure that we personally had lots of support.

I was disappointed. I felt ripped off that those three things were the only help he could give me. Perhaps I was unrealistic, but I thought that if my child had been diagnosed with cancer, diabetes, or anything else 'mainstream', surely I would have been given a blow-by-blow description of what would happen next, what could possibly happen, how much it would cost, how long it would take and what possible prognoses there were for the future?

Instead, I felt alone and floundering. Andrew and I drove home from grey Westmead, feeling more desperate and devastated than when we had come.

The rest of the day was a bit of a daze. Andrew had to go back to his classes, and I continued to look after the boys and headed to school later on to pick up Jasmine. It was life as normal on the outside, but every so often I made myself stop and think, "Autism. My child has autism." I had to do it to make myself grasp the reality of what was happening. My feelings felt detached from my body, and I worried that if I didn't make myself feel the weight of this, I would forget that it had happened. I needed it to be serious and real and close and heavy. It was as if the word 'autism' was a heavy, ugly, brown wool blanket that I had to wrap around me in order to feel its burden.

After a few hours I realised I had to tell my parents. They were overseas visiting people in remote parts of Africa for a month, so I found our mobile phone and sent them a text. It seemed ridiculous. My text sounded trite, and their answer sounded silly. How do you tell someone their grandchild has autism in four lines on a mobile phone? How do they text back with enough love and concern to make it ok?

We rang Andrew's parents too. But even the normal phone seemed inadequate for this kind of news. How can you tell someone over a plastic handset that you feel like the bottom has fallen out of your world?

In the evening I went to a jewellery-making craft night that had been organised by one of the Bible college women living around us. I am the sort of person who always honours a commitment, and I had said I would go several weeks previously. It didn't occur to me to stay home and cry. Perhaps I thought I needed the support of my friends. After all, they did know that the appointment had been in the morning. I should tell them the results.

The evening was strange. I talked light-heartedly about autism. "Yes, he has it for sure. Yes, the doctor's given us some things to do. Yes, I'm happy to have an answer."

A few of my friends had questions about ASD which I tried to answer, but I felt like an imposter. I didn't know enough about anything to be helpful. Looking back, I don't think I cried, but I felt like it.

The conversation moved on and around. I think we covered fridges and washing machines, birth control, jewellery design and housework that evening. I felt like two people—one participating happily and normally, and the other trying not to sob as I hugged myself on the edge of the group.

The next few weeks were similar. Wherever we went, people would ask what the result had been at the paediatrician. We would have five minutes of questions and answers about autism and what it would mean for Cameron and us, and then the conversations would circle around to other topics.

When it came back to autism, I tried to move it on. I felt uncomfortable with the focus on us and our big problem. It was like we were wrecking pleasant relationships and light-hearted exchanges talking about difficult subjects. I didn't want to be the depressed person who sucked pity out of everyone and then found herself being avoided because she wouldn't stop talking about ASD, but in all honesty, that was all I wanted to talk about. It was certainly all I talked to God about!

Autism had taken over my consciousness, and that was all I would want to know about for the next few months.

* * *

In my humble opinion... labels

Parents of children with difficulties can be roughly divided into two groups.

First, there are those who think a diagnosis 'labels' their child. They don't want their child to be defined by their difficulty and believe that if you focus on what is wrong, it will stick to the child for the rest of their life. They tend not to tell others that there is anything amiss with their child.

The other group is those parents who think a diagnosis is helpful because it defines what is wrong. They believe that if you know what is wrong, you can take steps to fix it. They think that it's not 'labelling' if it's true, and they'll talk freely about it.

I'm a parent in the second group. I have no problem whatsoever with referring to Cameron as 'a child with ASD' or 'mildly autistic'.

In fact in the first four years, I usually told people straight off, mostly because he was at an age where people expect him to interact normally with them. As he doesn't look different from others, it was not obvious that his developmental age is much younger than his physical age, so people were often surprised by his behaviour or responses.

(However, I wouldn't say it in front of him, I wouldn't say it to other children, and I would only say it to those adults who I believed would handle the information with respect and regard for him.)

As well, I find it helpful to talk about his autism, just for myself. It helps me work it all out and accept it all. And I think it gives others a realistic picture of my life and the challenges I'm facing right now.

5

Doing what the doctor said

I was very aware at this point that God was teaching me how to love. I didn't know, however, that this would mean more hard work than fuzzy feelings. I was thankful for a definite feeling of warmth towards my difficult child, but I still needed to find a way forward. It took a couple of weeks after the diagnosis before we realized that Cameron's treatment was going to be something we would have to handle ourselves.

Even though we were disappointed in the small amount of advice the paediatrician had given us, we had decided to do what he had told us. Andrew was still at college all day, writing final essays, and studying for exams, so the bulk of the task fell to me.

First I gathered up all my courage, took some deep breaths and rang the local autism association.

I've never been good at making phone calls. I spent my teenage years in a mud-brick house in a remote area of Pakistan, where our electricity supply was tenuous at best, and our phone line was non-existent. When you combine that with years at boarding school where I never even picked up a phone receiver, it's not surprising that I get nervous on the phone, even when I'm calling good friends.

Calling the autism association was a very scary prospect for me.

I felt young, new and very, very raw. I prayed aloud for help and wrote a few notes so that I'd actually be able to get something coherent out, but I was mostly hoping that whoever answered the phone was going to be able to hear the desperation and grief in my voice and give me some concrete steps to take in helping my boy.

It didn't happen.

The conversation went something like this.

Me: "Look, hi, I've been given this number by the paediatrician because my son's just been diagnosed with ASD and well, I'm kind of hoping you can help and I don't really know what I'm asking for?"

Lady on the phone: "So, who's done the diagnosing? What's his name? What did he tell you?"

Me: (with voice breaking up) "Our paediatrician. He said to call you people for some help."

Lady: "Oh. Well, where do you live?"

Me: (trying not to cry) "Right now we live in the inner west, but we'll be moving out of the area in a couple of months."

Lady: "Oh, I see. So you won't be around in Sydney then, which is where all of our services are. *Silence.* Well, there's a support group down where you're going. Shall I give you the number?"

Me: "Oh thank you. That would be great."

My nerves were somewhat appeased and I felt a little better, so I rang the number of the support group. Again, I wasn't sure what I was asking for, but inside I was hoping for a supportive fairy godmother who would speak kindly, understand my fears and offer me the help I was looking for. I started out tentatively.

Me: "Hi, Um, I've been given your number because you run a support group for autism? Would that be right?"

Woman on the phone: (in a very brusque voice) "Sorry, what?

Who gave you the number?"

Me: "Oh, er, the autism association? Do you have a support group or something? My son's just been diagnosed with autism, and I'm moving down there and I don't really know what to do or anything…"

Woman: "Hmm. You're the second person this week they've given the number to. I'll have to get some information or something. Yes, we meet. But they are mostly older children. How old is your child? Where are you moving to? When? Why?"

And so it went on. She was tough, loud and scary and when I got off the phone I burst into tears and crossed her off my list. The support the doctor had prescribed for us was not going to be found in that group.

The autism association had also given me a couple of government departments to ring for help and once I had decoded their acronyms, I looked up the numbers and started again. It wasn't much more help. Again, I received minimal information and very little understanding from them. It felt like I was being sent on a phone chase, hopping from number to number to find someone who knew how to help me. Unfortunately I never reached the end. After about five phone calls, I felt completely traumatised so I put the phone down in disgust and went and had a strong cup of tea and some serious amounts of chocolate to soothe my battered emotions.

So much for that. But I was still determined to fulfil all righteousness by doing what the paediatrician said, so my next step was speech therapy.

The local community speech therapist was free and I was able to get in pretty quickly now that we had a diagnosis. So Cameron and I went to some sessions with a young woman who asked me what his main issues and difficulties were.

I decided to focus on a couple of key difficulties and see if I could find some ways to manage our meltdown-filled days a little better.

"He has so much trouble making choices and decisions," I said. "Can you help me with that?"

The therapist had a few suggestions. She showed me how to do things like using pictures, sign language and choice boards.

"If he is choosing what colour t-shirt to wear in the morning, you can show him a picture of the red t-shirt and the blue t-shirt on the choice board and let him choose which one he wants," she said.

I was doubtful. If he ran away screaming when presented with the actual t-shirts, why was seeing a picture of them going to be any different? Besides, the thought of taking photographs of every item in his life, laminating them, putting Velcro on them, getting the right ones out at the right time, and then trying to stop him chewing and bending them just made me exhausted.

'If that's the best she's got, then she doesn't really have anything which solves the actual problem of his anxiety,' I thought.

In the middle of all of this, my father in law, the GP, had become doubtful about the original diagnosis.

"It must be something else," he was saying. "It can't be autism. Go and get a second paediatrician's opinion."

It seemed like a good idea. 'At the very least', I thought, 'I might see if she has some additional ideas on what to do. I'm getting nowhere from the first doctor's advice'.

The second paediatrician was a woman who agreed wholeheartedly with the first paediatrician in his diagnosis, adding this memorable phrase: "Well, your son's got absolutely atrocious social skills."

That hit home hard, especially because I thought Cameron had been pretty reasonable in her rooms.

But this doctor had no more advice on what to do to manage him, except a suggestion to go and see a psychologist who specialised in ASD.

"He's really good at practical solutions for challenging behaviour," she said.

I was willing to find some more money if I was going to find some answers and, with hope in my heart, I put Cameron in the car again and drove 75 minutes through the traffic, this time to the north of the city for a two-hour session.

Once again, it was disappointing.

The 'practical solutions' the paediatrician had talked about turned out to be an hour and three quarters of the psychologist talking at me, telling me all about autism and what autistic children typically do. I was annoyed. I had already done the research and I knew a lot of the theory he was trying to tell me about.

What I wanted were some specific answers for my particular problems with my individual child. What should I do to help him through the front door? How could I get him to eat a wider variety of food? Was there a way we could help him move away from his obsession with Thomas the Tank engine?

I was angry that I had dragged my poor little boy through traffic for hours for nothing. The psychologist had looked at him for literally two minutes and then, ironically, put a Thomas video on for him. It was a waste of his time and my time.

The final straw came when I went to leave. Outside the office, Cameron found some steps and wanted to climb up. I gave him a couple of minutes, but when it was time to go, he wouldn't get off them. He screamed and protested loudly and refused to come with me. The psychologist looked on while I spent ten minutes trying hopelessly to get Cameron to move while at the same time trying to avoid a major tantrum, but he offered no help. In desperation, I started to sing, "Let's walk together, let's walk together." After a few minutes or so Cameron took my hand and came relatively calmly with me to the car.

It was a depressing moment. I drove home angry and despondent, cursing the traffic, railing at the uselessness of so-called experts and praying for help in desperation.

But it was also an important moment.

So far, none of the doctors or professionals I had seen had offered anything that would actually work for my child and our family and make our chaotic lives any better.

I realised that we would have to be the ones who found the answers and judged the treatments. We would have to go looking for real help that would actually work.

"There must be something out there, Lord, " I asked in my prayer time. "You've got to help me find it. You have given us this child. Now let us be the ones who find out how to help him. Maybe that's the way I am going to love him best."

And so I turned, obsessively, to the internet. Surely someone out there had something that worked or knew something that would make a difference.

* * *

So what is ASD anyway?

Autism Spectrum Disorder (ASD) is a lifelong neuro-developmental condition which shows itself in three main areas: impairment in social interaction; impaired communication; and restricted and repetitive interests, activities and behaviours.

Autism spectrum disorders (ASDs) are are life-long, with no known cure. No-one knows exactly why they occur, although some researchers have identified genetic links.

It's called a 'spectrum' because no two ASD people look exactly the same. The range and severity of the difficulties people experience can vary enormously. Some people experience sensory disorders, or auditory processing disorders. They may also have co-existing learning difficulties.

Studies at the time of my son's diagnosis showed that 1 in 160 Australians were 'on the spectrum'. Numbers have risen since then to 1 in 70 Australians. The disorder affects four times as many boys as girls, and in different ways.

For more information, see www.aspect.org.au

6

Eggs and therapy

In a powerful, gut-wrenching image that had stuck in my brain, the unhelpful psychologist I saw had likened people to eggs. He said that a non-autistic person is like an egg with its shell filled with yolk and white as it is supposed to be. The egg looks like an egg and acts like an egg because it is a regular egg inside. The psychologist's argument was that autistic people are like empty egg shells. On the outside they appear normal, but inside there isn't a lot that is like a regular egg.

His idea of autism treatment was to teach the empty little shells skills so that they appear to be real eggs, even though they aren't.

A lot of the treatments that I read about propounded the same sorts of ideas, although not with such culinary imagery. It seemed that the accepted way to help autistic children was to teach them 'skills' or 'rules' they could remember. After that, they could practice applying the rules to every-day situations.

To me, it seemed like a paste-on solution. It was a solution that never really got to the main cause of the problems. It was a solution which was never going to help a fragile egg-shell survive the cracks of real life. I didn't think it was a loving solution. And it wasn't a solution I was prepared to accept for my son.

I wanted to look further, so I turned to that great library in the ether—the web. As any user of the internet knows, the great thing about it is that everything is out there for the finding. The bad thing is that there is no map that points you in the right direction, and you constantly have to sift out the bad or misleading information as you go.

My attitude was like a small terrier dog with a very large bone. I was one-eyed, tireless and unstoppable. Whatever free hours I had, I would spend on the computer. I used a ream of paper or more printing out my findings every night and then spent hours during the day re-reading it obsessively. Dinners became extremely basic and the housework deteriorated as I focused on my research.

My search was piecemeal, complicated and to a large extent, saw me chasing leads and following trails. I would get enthusiastic about something for a couple of days, but then I would look at it more closely, follow another link, find something else and get enthusiastic about that.

I discovered speech therapy, music therapy, auditory therapy, autism preschool, early intervention groups, physical therapy, sensory therapy, occupational therapy, special needs playgroups, nutritional therapy, heavy metals chelation, cranial osteopathic, holding therapy, homeopathy, naturopathy. Then there were the programs: ABA, Floortime, Sonrise and HANDLE to name a few.

Lots of it looked interesting. Some of it looked good. Most of it looked expensive.

It took me several links and an unrelated seminar to finally get to the Relationship Development Intervention Program (RDI), but once I read about it, I heaved an enormous sigh of relief. I felt like I had come home.

"This is the one," I told my husband who was by this time ready to be persuaded to anything. "This one makes the most sense. I like this one."

Like many other autism therapies, the program is the brainchild of a husband and wife team and comes out of the US, but its philosophy is different. Dr Gutstein and Dr Sheely, the founders, had taught children with autism for years using the accepted methods but was not convinced that the outcomes were all they could be. Dr Gutstein wanted to go deeper and find a solution that would have 'quality of life' as an outcome. He wanted to see children with autism grow up to be able to live flexible, messy, normal lives. He wanted them to have a real friend, hold a real job, enjoy a real relationship.

His theory was that there was no point re-inventing the wheel by making a program and deciding what and how and when to teach a skill, and then working out a new way to do it. He figured that typical childhood development followed a great pattern that obviously worked for most people. He wanted to follow that route, to go back and give children, teens and adults with autism a second chance at all the regular development they had missed out on first time around.

I was elated. If it worked, this was the sort of program I wanted Cameron to be part of. And if it didn't work, surely it couldn't be any worse than the therapies that wanted to treat him like an empty eggshell.

I was hoping, for the sake of our bank balance, that this program might be the sort of thing where I bought a book and worked through it myself. Unfortunately this wasn't the case. To do it properly, we had to sign up with an RDI consultant in Sydney and pay serious amounts of money for her expertise and advice, and of course, the program itself.

Andrew and I looked at each other and shrugged our shoulders when we got the letter outlining the costs we were up for.

"There's nothing else I can see that is going to be any better," I tried to persuade him. "Yes it's a lot of money. But quite honestly, it's less than a quarter of what we could pay for the other, more popular program. So it's fairly good value really. And anyway, what else are we going to do? I guess we can see it as investing in his education and his future. If he doesn't cost us now, he'll cost us huge amounts later on if he doesn't get any better."

We were lucky that we had the money to pay for it. We had sold our house before we went to Bible college so we had investments we could access. And access them we did.

In the two years before government funding for autism early intervention came in, we paid out thousands of dollars of our own money for Cameron's therapy.

I was anxious. Yes, I had done my research, but I wasn't a medical person or an autism professional. There was no proof and no double-blind published study in a medical journal that said 'this program will definitely cure your son'.

Sure, the program had lots of stories about how much children had improved, but no-one could give me a definitive, money-back guarantee. Were we doing something stupid? Were we going to be ripped off? Even though I had done as much research as I could do, I still didn't really know if I was falling for a scam, so I kept the amounts of money we were paying out strictly to myself. I didn't even tell my parents how much it was costing. I just wasn't sure if they might try to talk us out of doing it, out of concern for us, and I knew that I would find it hard to convince them that I was so desperate that I was going to try it anyway, no matter what it cost. (Of course, there was no program that had research behind it demonstrating that it would 'cure any child' or show quality of life gains. No program, therapy or drug offers money back guarantees for any medical condition and if they do, it's probably a scam!)

We had to wait a little while before we could officially start with our RDI consultant, but in the meantime, she gave us some advice to follow to try to get things moving.

The first thing we had to do was something that went against my personality, my experience and my desires. I read it and groaned at my husband.

"We're supposed to slow down!" I complained.

"You're going to find this really hard!" he grinned.

Slowing down meant not only slowing down the pace I moved at, but also slowing down the craziness in my head that was telling me, 'you have to do everything you can and as much as you can for Cameron right now'.

There is a real temptation with a child with special needs to try anything and everything all the time because surely something is bound to work. You couldn't live with yourself if you didn't do the very thing that just might have some great effect, and you don't know unless you try, right?

RDI's theory is that autism remediation takes time and happens slowly. The children need rest and routine so that their brains can re-learn normal development. If parents are too busy whisking their children off to this and that, they can't spend the time they need with them, and the children don't have time to process what they are learning. A child will not do well with RDI if their family runs at a frenetic pace.

This was probably the hardest thing I had to face. I have always gone at 130 miles an hour. I work hard and fast, and then I collapse. I like to schedule lots of things in. I like rushing. I like to achieve aims and goals. I like being busy. It defines me and makes me feel important.

Could I do this? Could I really put things aside, say no to commitments and make a conscious effort to have a more relaxed, less crowded life?

It hurt to do, but I knew I had to do it. I love my son more than I love the things I do. I meant it when I said I would do anything so that he could get better, and when push came to shove, I was able to give up things I loved to do so that I could focus on him and help him. Over the next few months, I said no to writing a new book, pared down my church commitments, sold my cloth nappy business and packed away my sewing machine and cut down on the stress in his life.

It helped me to keep remembering the words I had had from God about learning to love. When I felt bereft, stretched and disoriented, I was thankful that at least I knew what it was all for. "OK, I get it. This is all happening for a reason," I could say to God. I believed it, and I could see how all of these things would work for good in the long run.

The second thing we had to do was not as emotionally demanding, but it challenged us in the way we related to all our children. What we had to do was to change our language.

In general conversation, studies have shown that about 80 per cent of our speech is declarative. That means that we make comments or observations. We describe something. We point out something. We talk with someone about what we've been doing.

The other 20 per cent of our general communication is instrumental. We speak to obtain a response, usually by asking a question or giving an instruction.

Often, though, when adults talk to children, we end up reversing this. We ask a lot of questions and give a lot of directions. But it's not the way we would normally speak to other people.

The RDI principle is to model normal language for our children with ASD and keep to 80 per cent declarative and 20 per cent instrumental speech as much as possible. Instead of requiring a response, we are inviting a response.

And in keeping with piece of advice number one, we also try to slow down the conversation and leave lots of gaps to encourage original thought.

"Count to 30 or even more when you share an observation," our consultant advised. "It gives him time to process, and leaves it open for his own response."

Count to 30? I'm a fast talker and a fast thinker. I thought counting to 30 might just kill me.

Before we started RDI, I might say something to Cameron like, "What colour is that flower?" It was a ridiculous question, but I was so desperate for him to respond in some way to me, that I would feel better if he gave me the 'right' answer. It somehow proved to me that he wasn't as lacking as I thought he was.

He responded the way I wanted here and there, but more often he would resist answering and would yell instead because he could sense I was putting pressure on him. When I didn't get the answer I wanted, I'd change the question or ask it again. I was basically drowning him with the noise of my voice and making it impossible for him to process what I was saying and respond to me.

The day after I learned about changing my language, I tried it out.

"Oh wow—there's a flower over there," I said to Cameron. I shut my mouth and counted to 30.

At 28 he said, "red flower".

I felt tears in my eyes. It was our first real conversation. And it was a massive breakthrough. Maybe things were finally on the right track.

7

Holland, and why I didn't want to join the secret club

As I was burning up the internet looking for help for Cameron, I discovered a government-funded early intervention service for children with all sorts of special needs, including autism. It looked good, it was free and it was local—just a 15 minute drive away.

I rang up to find out that there was (of course) a waiting list for individualised help, but that Cameron and I were welcome to attend their weekly 'open playgroup'. I decided I should try it, so I wrestled him and the baby into the car one Thursday morning, found a parking spot in the narrow streets and ventured gingerly in.

As playgroups go, it was terrific. There was lots of great play equipment and interesting toys. It was set up beautifully and three friendly helpers welcomed all the mothers and their children, joined in the play, and then ran a wonderful story time at the end.

But it was a depressing and a stretching experience. Playgroups are supposed to be fun, but I felt like I had suddenly joined a secret misery club that I really didn't want to be part of.

I had gone in thinking, "This is for all sorts of 'special needs' children. I'll find out that Cameron doesn't really fit in here. He won't have special needs in comparison with the other children. They'll be much worse than he is. I'll probably feel quite sorry for the other parents here."

But as I looked around, and recognised my own anxiety and frustration and sadness on the face of every other parent there, my heart sank as I realised that I was just the same as them. I and my child were now part of the special needs world.

And the worst thing was: Cameron was not the 'best' one there. It's true, I could look around and see kids who had more obvious and visible problems than his, but by and large, he fitted in quite well.

I went home sad, diminished and shocked all over again. Diagnosis of Cameron's autism was one thing. Joining the ranks of people I had previously tried to avoid in life because I felt unable to open my eyes to their pain and suffering—well that was a whole new ballgame.

My mind was racing all that day. Memories flooded back to me as I tried to understand how I felt.

I remembered back to antenatal classes when I was first pregnant with Jasmine. The whole room was full of excited young parents-to-be, asking earnest questions about dealing with labour and birth and nappies and breastfeeding.

"You probably need to think about how you might cope if something goes wrong," the midwife said to the group at one point. "What do you think your worst-case scenario might be?"

A brown-haired woman put up her hand. "For me, I'm terrified of having a caesarean. What will I do if that happens?"

I gave a grimace. I, too, never wanted to have a caesarean. That would be both scary and painful—two states that I had always tried to avoid inflicting on myself.

"Yes, that would be hard," said the midwife. "But I'm talking about with the baby. I'm talking about if something is wrong with the baby."

There was a collective stillness. No-one moved. No-one said anything. We lowered our eyes and tried to avoid the nurse's gaze. It was unthinkable that there could be anything wrong with our babies. Even though I'm not superstitious, I didn't want to think about the possibilities. It felt as if by admitting that something could happen to our babies, I might unknowingly open the doors to tragedy.

"Well, look, if something happens, which is pretty unlikely anyway, you'll deal with it as you come to it," said the nurse brightly, trying to get some life back into the discussion. "You obviously don't want to chat about it, so let's talk about giving baby a bath."

The good mood returned to the room and we giggled again as the midwife handed around baby dolls and led us to the sink.

More memories came racing back into my mind.

I thought about a little girl with profound deafness and facial disfigurement who had attended our church when Jasmine was a baby. I used to watch her, surreptitiously and from afar, trying to understand what had happened to her. I avoided her parents because I didn't want to know more. If I got too close, I might have to share their grief and open my eyes to the possibility that such a tragedy could possibly happen to me. Their family was part of a different world—a separate group of people, who experienced things that I hoped would never come into my life.

I remembered a young man with severe cerebral palsy and spasticity who came to our university church. He was unable to walk or speak or take care of himself in any way. He communicated using a board. It was painfully slow to talk to him, and anyway, I never knew what to say. How can you ask, "So, how's your day?" when you can see that his day is full of things that would make me depressed beyond words? Plus, he drooled and laughed too loudly and was really hard to understand. I tried to avoid him too, and then tried to rationalise the guilt that came from avoiding him.

I remembered kids at school who were just that little bit 'different', who didn't relate well, or who had odd habits. Being friends with the strange kids was exhausting and tiring and called for more energy than I wanted to give. I felt sorry for them, but still avoided them as much as I could because I didn't need the extra stress and I didn't want them to cling to me as their only friend.

These were all people I classed in a category 'over there'. I didn't want to understand them or get close to them, and I argued to myself that they probably coped just fine in their own lives and they didn't really need me to get involved. If I heard their story, I might express a sympathetic line like, "Oh, that must be so hard," but then I would subconsciously cut off the sympathy and close my ears and eyes to them so that I could get on with my life.

That day, I realised that I was now part of the group 'over there'. I cried and cried. I felt as if all the categories I had set up for myself so that I could have a happy and carefree life had been demolished. My identity had changed and my future life was going to change too. I practiced saying the words, "I have a child who has special needs," so that I could see how it felt but the words seemed to be stuck halfway down my throat.

Of course, I entertained the thoughts that everyone thinks: *Am I being punished for something? Is this just payback for the way I treated the disabled people and the 'oddballs' in my life?* It took a lot of convincing myself that no, this was neither punishment nor payback. I had to keep remembering that all of this would end up being good for me—teaching me how to love more honestly and more truly. Remembering that made me less bitter, but no less miserable. It was just such a painful way to learn the lesson.

To do the right thing for my beautiful boy, however, I went back to the playgroup.

It took me a few weeks to get up the courage to talk to any of the other parents at any length. Part of my fear was in having to confront the elephant in the room which was the subject of their child's disability. It seemed rude to ask, "So, why are *you* here?" with a wink at their child, and yet it was the obvious point of reference that had brought us together. I desperately wanted to know what was wrong with *their* kid so that I could compare with *my* kid, but it would have been completely offensive.

Finally, after enough small smiles and off-hand remarks, I got talking to a mother whose little boy seemed very much like Cameron to me. Jen also had a babe in arms like Max, but to me she appeared so much more together and controlled than I felt.

It turned out our boys were nearly the same age, and had been diagnosed with ASD in about the same week. We had something in common.

Jen was refreshingly honest in what she said about her feelings about autism. While I had generally kept my anger inside me and tried to at least appear positive and as though I was a good Christian who was trusting God about it up to this point, she quite openly said what she thought.

One of the first things we were both given by the cheerful and very nurturing playgroup staff was a photocopied paper with a story called 'Welcome to Holland' on it. It was an allegory, likening the process of having a child to taking a journey. We prepare excitedly for what we think will be our healthy, normal child, much like we would prepare with anticipation for a trip to Italy. We picture all the exciting things we'll do and see, and we dream about the joys and thrills of Italy.

However, once we get off the plane and land, we discover that we've arrived, not in Italy, but in Holland. It's different. It's not what we prepared for. At first, we are very disappointed. We wander around, looking at windmills and things that we didn't choose to see. As time goes on, though, we realise that Holland has a lot to offer. Things we might have never chosen for ourselves. We miss Italy, but we can see that Holland isn't worse, it's just different.

I read it over and tried to be hopeful and see past my own grief at landing in Holland. But Jen said, "I don't care what this says. It's still shit, whether they serve it with a silver spoon or not."

I gasped at her. And then I grinned. Sometimes love means being honest and admitting what you think you shouldn't say. It was how I felt too, even though I was trying desperately to be good and nice about it. We were both stuck here with children with major problems and we felt mad about it. We weren't just angry because of what we knew our children were going to suffer in life, but we were angry because *we* were the ones who were here, doing the work of helping our children. Our lives were being changed forever, not just our children's lives. Jen expressed it more clearly than I had dared to thus far.

"Look," she said. "The dads care, but in the end, it's us mums who get to carry the crap. Because we're the ones who will, because we know that no-one else will. It's bloody awful, but we have to do it."

We smiled at each other. I still believed that God was working in me. But I hadn't been able to say how horrible I felt yet. Telling the truth felt better. And having a friend to experience it with made things slightly better still.

I had landed in Holland, and joined a secret misery club. It took my breath away, and threw my life upside down, but at least I wasn't there alone.

* * *

Welcome to Holland

I am often asked to describe the experience of raising a child with a disability—to try to help people who have not shared that unique experience to understand it, to imagine how it would feel. It's like this...

When you're going to have a baby, it's like planning a fabulous vacation trip—to Italy. You buy a bunch of guide books and make your wonderful plans. The Coliseum. Michelangelo's David. The gondolas in Venice. You may learn some handy phrases in Italian. It's all very exciting.

After months of eager anticipation, the day finally arrives. You pack your bags and off you go. Several hours later, the plane lands. The stewardess comes in and says, "Welcome to Holland."

"Holland?!?" you say. "What do you mean Holland?? I signed up for Italy! I'm supposed to be in Italy. All my life I've dreamed of going to Italy."

But there's been a change in the flight plan. They've landed in Holland and there you must stay.

The important thing is that they haven't taken you to a horrible, disgusting, filthy place, full of pestilence, famine and disease. It's just a different place.

So you must go out and buy new guide books. And you must learn a whole new language. And you will meet a whole new group of people you would never have met.

It's just a different place. It's slower-paced than Italy, less flashy than Italy. But after you've been there for a while and you catch your breath, you look around.... and you begin to notice that Holland has windmills....and Holland has tulips. Holland even has Rembrandts.

But everyone you know is busy coming and going from Italy... and they're all bragging about what a wonderful time they had there. And for the rest of your life, you will say "Yes, that's where I was supposed to go. That's what I had planned."

And the pain of that will never, ever, ever, ever go away... because the loss of that dream is a very, very significant loss.

But... if you spend your life mourning the fact that you didn't get to Italy, you may never be free to enjoy the very special, the very lovely things ... about Holland.

By Emily Perl Kingsley, 1987 found at http://www.our-kids.org/Archives/Holland.html

I also love 'Welcome to Beirut' by Susan F. Rzucidlo, found at http://www.bbbautism.com/beginners_beirut.htm

8

Going all domestic

The next thing God taught me about love was that sometimes it means I have to stretch myself and do things I would never choose to do ordinarily.

In this case, it meant cooking.

Cameron and I started to hang out with Jen and her boys at their place. It was good to get to know someone coping with the same challenges that I was facing. Plus she was a great source of information.

One of her big interests was what's known in the autism world as 'bio-med'. It's a nutritional approach which argues that giving supplements as well as a diet rich in the things the child is lacking will help brain function.

The second time we went to visit she showed me an enormous chest freezer she had bought to store all her son's special food in, rather than having to cook something different for him every night.

"Have you heard of the gluten-free, casein-free diet?" she asked. "I think it's going to really help."

"I don't even know what casein is!" I laughed, and then groaned. "I'm so not up for changing his diet. I'm just not that mother who spends her time cooking everything. I think I'd go crazy."

It was true. I was neither enthusiastic nor accomplished in the kitchen and besides, I had heard that biomed supplements cost families thousands. We were already spending more than we could afford and I had no intention of going down that route.

However, after our RDI consultant met Cameron, one of the first things she mentioned was looking into diet.

"I don't normally recommend this but I think he will benefit from it," she said.

One of his problems was a recurring rash around his mouth, which he licked continually all day and night. He also loved putting metal in his mouth. My keys were constantly dripping with drool as a result.

"He might have a mineral deficiency," she said. "It's something to try, anyway."

I didn't know what to do about this. It looked like a huge area to investigate. And how was I to find the right doctor after all my negative experiences with paediatricians and psychologists so far?

Thankfully, Jen had the right information. She had found a GP with a particular interest in autistic children. And even better for our hip pocket, he bulk-billed! There would be no expense for us.

We made the appointment. It was an interesting experience. His practice is in Sydney's most multicultural suburb, and his grotty little waiting room was filled with people of all colours, speaking in many different languages, in different ethnic dress. After waiting for an hour, Cameron was more than ready to be seen, and finally we went in to meet the doctor.

He talked at great length about essential mineral depletion, under-methylation, digestive enzyme support and a lot of other complicated terms that I could not remember or replicate for anyone else. But he did it with such authority that I believed everything he said and decided to do everything he suggested.

At the end of the consultation, he filled out several prescriptions for supplements and ordered a battery of tests. As he told me the costs of each one, my heart sank, but I thought, 'Well, I'll try this all once. At least we can see what happens.'

First on the list was to get a urine test done.

I was slightly worried about collecting the sample because at this stage, Cameron was still wearing nappies all day. I rang the collection centre and said, "I'm getting this test done but my son's not toilet trained. What can I do?"

"Easy," said the cheerful girl on the other end. "Just come in and get a special collection bag for it. Then once you've got the sample, bring it in for testing."

I drove the 15 minutes to their office to get the cute little collection bag. It was rather ingenious. You literally stick it on the appropriate place, put on the child's nappy and wait.

Being a little worried about how Cameron would react to a bag stuck on his privates however, I decided that the only way I could get it on and keep it on without him ripping it off in a fit of rage would be to put it on while he was asleep and collect the wee overnight. I stuck it on, congratulated myself on my clever thinking and went to bed.

The next morning we had an appointment to get his blood test done, so Andrew and I dropped Jasmine off at school and went up with both boys, urine sample in tow. Unfortunately due to my bad memory for roads and places, we got lost, arrived at the clinic three minutes late, 'missed' our appointment and then had to sit in the waiting room for another 45 minutes.

By the time we got in for the blood test, Cameron was not in a mood to co-operate. There was no way he was going to sit still so that a needle could be pushed into his arm, and he needed to be held down. Reinforcements were called, and I was firmly told by the nurse to leave the room once I started to cry at all the kicking and screaming that was going on.

So I wasn't feeling too happy when after everything was over, I handed the nurse the urine sample and she said, with disdain in her voice, "I can't accept that. It's not frozen."

"Not frozen?" said I.

"Yes. It has to be frozen. And is it the *second* void?" she asked.

"Second void?" I repeated blankly.

"Yes—the second wee of the day. It has to be the second wee of the day," she said.

No-one told me that on the phone, I thought grimly. And taking my urine sample, I stalked out, prepared to bring one back later.

That day, I managed to catch his 'second wee' in another little collection bag. With glee, I stuffed it into the freezer and in the morning I was back with my frozen sample in an esky.

The junior nurse looked at me mildly apologetically. "Um, we tried to ring you, but we'd already sent your phone number away with the paperwork from the blood work. We can't accept your sample. Sorry."

It turns out this time I had 'forgotten' (their word, not mine) to catch the sample in the dark, wrap it in silver foil (shiny side out, dull side in), then freeze it.

I went home. I was determined not to be defeated. The next day I caught the second wee of the day in darkness. I wrapped it in foil (shiny side out, dull side in) and I popped it in the freezer. The following morning, I drove back up to their office, lugging an esky.

"We can't accept that sample," said the aggressive senior nurse.

"You didn't mix it with the acid. You weren't listening," she said.

"Excuse me," I said, my blood beginning to boil. "I've been listening ever since the first phone call. You'd better tell me *exactly* what I have to do and I will do it. I have been following the instructions I've been given ever since the first day!"

We went through it twice. I went home and again, did what I was told. I caught the second wee of the day in the dark, poured it into a little container with acid, put the lid on tightly, shook the container, wrapped it in foil (shiny side out, dull side in), put it in the freezer. And then I took it back to the office the next day.

The senior nurse looked at me blankly. "But it's frozen," she said. "We can't take that."

"Yes, it's frozen," I said at high volume. "It's been caught in the dark. It's been mixed with acid. It's wrapped with foil. It is frozen, just like you wanted."

"But... we always freeze it on dry ice," she said. Then she added, defensively, "Well, I'll send it in, but I can't promise that you'll get the correct result. You might be wasting your money."

My lessons in love failed at this point. I felt like sticking my tongue out at her as she stalked down the hallway, taking my son's precious urine sample with her.

But the saga was over, and soon I was back in the exotic but rundown surgery, waiting to see the doctor about the results.

I understood some of what he said. I didn't understand a lot of it as well. But my layperson's version of it all was essentially that the brain does not stand alone. Gut function affects the brain. Nutrition affects the brain. Levels of copper and zinc and other minerals affect the brain. So a neurological disorder can be helped by treating other systems in the body.

My grasp on the theory was shaky, but practically, I was

delighted to go home with a list of things to do that would help.

The first thing was to bite the bullet and put Cameron on a gluten-free and casein-free diet, like Jen had originally suggested. (Casein, it turned out was milk protein). My heart sank when I heard it, but I could understand why I needed to do it.

I started out by looking at what he did eat. It was a bit of a shock to realise that he only ate fifteen different foods. That's a fairly limited diet for a three year-old. The entire list included: pasta, beef sausages, ham, cheese, vegemite sandwiches, apples, watermelon, cereal, milk, sultanas, crackers, chocolate cake, yoghurt, ice cream and tomato sauce, if indeed, tomato sauce is actually a food. You'll notice there were no vegetables in the list.

Getting rid of the gluten was the first challenge. These days, enough people are on celiac diets so that you can find wheat substituted products in the supermarket. Some of them taste a bit dodgy (and my daughter point blank refused to even try gluten free food) but most of them are pretty good. The milk part was harder to substitute as many gluten free foods still have milk solids and casein in them.

I looked back at my list of foods. Every single item except apples, watermelon and tomato sauce needed to be modified or replaced on the GF/CF diet.

But then I hit another snag. The doctor said that Cameron's mineral levels were out of whack. He had incredibly high copper and really low zinc levels, which causes 'under-methylation' of the brain and the autistic symptoms.

"He's got to avoid foods with copper in them," the doctor told me, in the middle of a long and convoluted paragraph. I grabbed onto it as something practical I understood and wrote it down.

But then I had to work out which foods contained copper. It turns out ham and pork have high levels. Dried fruits and chocolate are also culprits. And soy is another copper-rich food. So if I substituted cow's milk for soy milk and yoghurt for soy yoghurt, I would be pumping even higher doses of copper into his body.

I crossed off the high copper foods on my list and was left with this:

GF pasta, GF beef sausages, GF sandwiches, apples, watermelon, *GF cereal, rice milk, GF crackers* and tomato sauce.

It wasn't exactly the world's most balanced or varied diet.

If that wasn't enough, I then started looking at ADHD, and the recommended diet for that. This was different from the autism diet. It removed all preservatives and colours and foods with salicylates in them. If I followed that too, I'd have to take out apples, sausages, and the all important tomato sauce.

The doctor had suggested introducing more, different nutritious foods into his diet.

"Look, I'm all for that," I said. "The big problem is that I cannot get him to eat them, no matter what I do."

"You've just got to be perseverative," he said and moved on to the next topic.

I'd never even heard the word before but I could guess what it meant. I sighed. It seemed so hard to keep going when Cameron literally ran away from the dinner table in hysterics at the sight of something new on his plate.

I searched the diet books I'd been reading for solutions. How did these people make their fussy autistic children eat broth, green peas, organic chicken, wheat germ and freshly squeezed juices? From all I could tell, there was a lot of screaming involved. And I was guessing it wasn't all from the child.

The guilt began to set in. I knew his body needed good nutrition, but I just couldn't force the stuff down his throat. He was so anxious that he just wouldn't cope. The best I could do was try to find reasonably healthy alternatives and offer them to him with my fingers and toes crossed and with a few desperate prayers. More often than not, he rejected them, but occasionally I had success.

I became the queen of the hidden vegetable. I made fresh carrot juice and mixed it in with his drinks. I added grated zucchini, (skins removed because they're green) eggs and almond meal to gluten free bread mixes. I even got my local butcher to add pureed vegies to a batch of GF sausages. My greatest triumph came when I bought a doughnut maker and managed to get him to eat doughnuts made with banana and sweet potato—and lots of icing, of course.

For the next year and a half, my favourite kind of shopping was at health food stores and my ongoing project was to try to create healthy food that might, just might, get eaten. The bad days were when I threw out concoctions that failed through my inadequate kitchen skills, or were just plain rejected. The good days were when he ate an egg, or a doughnut, or drank a mouthful of carrot-infested juice.

The bad days outnumbered the good days by about ten to one.

That was the food. Then there were the supplements.

These were a mixed bunch. The digestive enzymes that he was supposed to eat with every meal were yummy little things, just like lollies, and luckily Cameron had never had an issue eating lollies. The Omega6 oils could be rubbed straight into his skin—another easy thing to do. The zinc-enriched mega-vitamin liquid, on the other hand was completely foul and a nightmare to administer.

Cameron refused to swallow capsules of the stuff, even though I tried every trick I could find, including ordering a specially-designed, capsule-taking drinking cup from the US. He quite sensibly refused to take it as liquid on a spoon or a dropper because it tasted worse than bile. I tried mixing it with a flavoured masking fluid the chemist supplied and then tried to hide that in vegemite, tomato sauce and juice throughout the day, but it was still very difficult to predict if he'd eat it, and if he'd end up getting the right dose throughout the day.

After a number of months of fighting and tears and tantrums, I decided that just like forcing food down his throat, making him take the medicine was raising his anxiety levels too much, which was being counter-productive to the remediation of his autism. I stopped administering it. To be honest, I'm not sure I saw the effect of it anyway.

What I did see a result with was the removal of the gluten and casein. Cameron's eyes became less glassy and more alive. He seemed to understand more and communicate more. He took some steps forward and achieved some milestones. I could see this would be something worth pursuing in the long-term.

From being a reluctant 'diet mum' at the beginning, I followed the nutrition trail vigorously for about two and a half years. I went to seminars, read books, and learned as much as I could. I believed it all and was so truly convinced that it worked that for a long time, at every meal time and snack time I felt hugely guilty because the fact remained that even after all my efforts, he still wouldn't eat good stuff. He continued to refuse most meat and all vegetables, eggs and fish. He continued to love sugar and chips and lollies and ice-blocks.

After a few years of guilt, I decided that perhaps I needed to give myself a break. We stuck with the GF-CF diet, and I provided balanced meals, but I was no longer beating myself up over it. I could get back to it later, after all. There were still too many other things I had to deal with.

**

Diet and the bio-med approach

Some people love it while others hate it, and the experts certainly argue about it but 'diet as therapy' for autism and ADHD is certainly out there in many forms. I've become a big fan. The year after I first wrote and published the first edition of this book, we had amazing results with a different doctor who has a particular interest in this area. She took a broader approach than the first doctor and looked at things like supplements, detoxification and digestive health. She also sent Cameron off for auditory processing testing. He started sound therapy and has had great results with that too. We've now been seeing her for years, and I credit her with many, many of our breakthroughs. As Cameron has gotten older, he has begun to take more and more responsibility for his own health. Recently, he even chose to try two new vegetables!

Get started on your 'bio-med' journey with these sites: www.mindd.org, www.breakingtheviciouscycle.info and www.gapsdiet.com

9

Up and down and round and round with RDI

For about four or five months from the date of Cameron's diagnosis, everything had been a whirl of activity. If I had to draw a diagram of the progress we made, it would be a long arrow pointing in a single direction. Things changed, however. Now instead of our progress being an arrow, it was more like a spiral. It seemed like we just kept on doing the same things, over and over again. I couldn't always see the changes that were happening, and I didn't always feel positive about it, but the lesson that God was teaching me was that love must persevere.

Cameron's preschool teachers were great at letting me know how he was going.

His first ever visit there, two months after his diagnosis had been for an interview with the preschool director. We were aiming to have him begin the following year, in about four months time. It was not an auspicious start.

He spent the hour playing outside in the freezing cold, refusing to come inside. He would hardly engage with the preschool director, and when he fell in the mud and made his track pants wet, he began to yell in protest. After he violently and loudly refused every possible different pair of spare trousers that the preschool had in their back room, we piled him, wet, dirty and still yelling, back into the car, apologised to the director and headed home.

It's not surprising that over the next few months, I became a little worried about how he was going to manage at preschool.

The director was a little worried as well, even though she didn't tell me at the time. But her opinion changed drastically after his first month there.

At the end of the preschool day at pick up time, I would always try to catch her eye and have a little chat about Cameron's day. Had he survived? Had the staff survived? Were there any good things to report? Anything I should be concerned about?

And then, one day, just a few weeks in, she said something that completely floored me.

"I am amazed at Cameron," she began. "When I first met him last August I wondered what I was letting myself in for. He's a different child now. I can honestly say I have never seen a child like this make so much progress and change so much."

It was so gratifying to hear her opinion. I knew that he had improved a lot in the seven months since his diagnosis. But seeing progress with your own child can be like trying to watch him grow. It's so slow that it's almost impossible to see. Often it's easiest to see it through other people's eyes.

What had made the difference? I was convinced that it was mostly down to the Relationship Development Intervention Program.

Once I'd discovered RDI and done some reading, I was ready to start. That hour. That morning. That day. Immediately.

Unfortunately the consultant we'd booked in to see wasn't available for another month. I was amazed that she didn't seem to see the urgency of our situation and see us straight away, but I had no other route to take, so I resigned myself to the waiting process. In the meantime, I got right on to doing the things she had suggested first off to do.

First of all, we had to watch a DVD all about the program. I was ready, with pen and notebook in hand, to watch the entire thing in one sitting. Too bad it was five hours long.

"I'm really sorry," said my husband after the first half hour. "I am interested, you know that, but this is really boring. I'm not sure I can do much more of this tonight. Plus, it's so technical and all these big words are rolling together in my head."

I was annoyed, but I turned the DVD off and re-read my notes feverishly for the rest of the evening.

It was the smart thing to do. There was so much good information in the DVD that we both needed time to digest it. If I had rushed ahead in my usual state of panic, I wouldn't have taken nearly as much in. And we both had a lot to learn.

The first thing that hit us right between the eyes was the fact that what little research has been done on the effects of autism all shows that even supposedly 'high-functioning' autistic adults have huge trouble living normal lives in society. It's safe to say that less than 12 per cent of autistic adults hold down a job, live independently and have at least one friend.

It wasn't a happy start to the DVD. But it was a good way to realistically look at what we were up against. The real gold came when the DVD explained what the actual problems of autism were, and then told us how the RDI program can treat them.

This was what I'd been waiting for. This wasn't an 'empty egg' paste-on type of solution.

I began to look at Cameron in a different way. I could see much more clearly the things he was missing and unable to do, and now I was beginning to understand why.

For example, after a few sessions of DVD watching, Andrew and I grasped the difference between static intelligence and dynamic intelligence.

To give a simple example, static intelligence is when you can recite a whole lot of big words and what they mean. Dynamic intelligence is knowing the words, but also knowing how, when and where to use them. It's about being able to gauge whether an audience will understand them if you're standing up to give a presentation, or whether they will think you are pretentious and snobby for using them.

Dynamic intelligence is juggling context, meaning, emotions, culture, expectations and desires, needs and wants when answering a question. Does two plus two always equal four? In a static system, of course it does. In a dynamic system, it might not, if we're pretending in a fabulous game that twos are really threes in magic maths land. Or if we're speaking in metaphors and discussing the fact that life has a lot of grey areas for which there are no definitive answers.

So far in his life, Cameron had acquired a good number of static skills. He could count, spell and read. He could name all the colours and shapes, and (of course) knew the numbers and colours and names of all the Thomas the Tank Engine characters.

People were impressed by him when he did these things. I had heard more than once, "Wow, your son is really smart."

I was impressed too, and hoped that his displays of knowledge would somehow make up for the other problems he seemed to have.

Unfortunately, I didn't realise that his static intelligence would never be able to help him to live in the real world. Knowing what colours and shapes are would not help him to decide how to find his way through problems and dilemmas. They could not help him negotiate personal relationships.

Once again, I was a little shocked to see just how much my beautiful son was missing. But I was hopeful that here was a program which could treat his dynamic intelligence deficits. RDI recognised the problem and had a solution which would help my son to live a meaningful life.

Slowing down to watch the DVD was just a taste of things to come. I found it hard to grasp that it would be much better in the long run for Cameron if I could relax a bit and get out of 'crisis mode'.

Being in perpetual crisis is exhausting and unworkable. You can't think creatively, and you have no energy to do anything more than react. But being an effective parent is about going beyond the reacting phase, and acting intentionally with your child.

RDI parents constantly say, "it's a marathon, not a sprint," when they talk about working with their children. Personally, I was never a good long distance runner and I've always had a short attention span. This was going to be something that would demand serious changes from me.

When we finally, officially began the program in earnest, the first thing that our consultant did was a big assessment, spread out over several days.

The first part was an ADOS test. The Autism Diagnostic Observation Schedule is a test which can help a clinician diagnose autism or Asperger's syndrome. We parents were invited to sit in the room and watch while the consultant interacted with Cameron. It was as much as I could do to keep my bottom on the chair and my mouth quiet. It was absolutely shocking to see how ineffective my beautiful son's communication was, and how little he could relate to the consultant. I didn't realise that I had spent much of the last year stepping in and 'fixing' things for him, trying to make him appear more socially successful than he really was.

The next part of the assessment was where I and Andrew took turns with him doing different tasks the consultant gave us. She watched from the next room via a remote camera. Again, it was hard. We felt incompetent and angry with ourselves, seeing our own failures even while we were hoping to prove what great parents we were, and what a good relationship we had with our child.

From there, the consultant worked with him individually to get an even better picture of where he was at, and where our starting point should be.

After that, it was a case of sit, listen and learn. We had to learn to invite, rather than command, a response. We had to learn how to frame our activities appropriately and to interpret accurately where the breakdowns in communication came from. We had to learn how to change our language. We had to learn to help him calm himself down. We had to learn child development concepts and terminology.

Even my husband, who by this time had three university degrees and two diplomas, felt like he was back in kindergarten, starting from the very beginning. So many of our parenting practices had to be re-evaluated, thrown out and then replaced. It was an overwhelming time.

But it was beginning to work. And it was saving my sanity.

At the time of diagnosis, Cameron's language had been mostly confined to 'scripts'. He learned phrases from books, TV shows and CDs and repeated them over and over and over and over and over and over and...

That would have been irritating enough, except that most of the time he wanted a response from me, again and again and again and again and...

So a typical conversation would go like this.

Him: Thomas the Tank Engine, mum. Thomas the Tank Engine, mum. Thomas, mum. Thomas the Tank Engine, mum. Thomas the Tank Engine, mum. Thomas the...

Me (in a resigned voice): Yes, Thomas. Thomas is a train.

Him: Thomas has six small wheels mum. Thomas has six small wheels mum. Thomas has six small wheels. Six small wheels mum.

Me (in a slightly more irritated resigned voice): Yes he does. He's got wheels! Wow! Six of them. Imagine that!

Him: Thomas the Tank Engine, mum. Thomas the Tank Engine, mum. Thomas the Tank Engine mum.....

And so it went on, for much of the day.

I was in a dilemma about it. On one level, he was communicating with me, even if it was a scripted phrase so I didn't want to just ignore him. In any case, I couldn't ignore him. He rose in volume every minute that I didn't answer!

Our RDI consultant suggested two, very practical things.

"Usually what I recommend in these cases is ipod therapy," she said to me.

I tried to sound a little knowledgeable. "Um, an ipod for him?" I ventured.

"No. An ipod for you!" she laughed. "Every time he scripts, your heartbeat increases and you breathe more rapidly with the frustration. If you have something peaceful playing in your ears, you're not going to hear him unless you really need to. And when you do respond, you're not going to add tension to the situation. He'll give up demanding you to hear him eventually if he doesn't get a response from you."

I tried it and it worked. Even though it didn't stop his scripting, I felt happier, and surprisingly it did reduce Cameron's demands on me a fair bit.

The second solution was to start chanting or singing. When our consultant told me about this, I was a little sceptical. Could it really work?

Amazingly, it did. When Cameron came out with his usual scripted words, I took control of them myself by turning them into a song.

Our conversations started to go like this.

Him: "Thomas the tank Engine mum. Thomas the Tank Engine."

Me: (in a rhythmic kind of way) "Thomas, the Tank Engine, Thomas the Tank.

Thomas the Tank Engine. Thomas—Yeah!

Thomas is a train, Thomas is a train,

Thomas is a train. A cute little train—yeah!"

I found that he would start to look at my face and process what I was doing. He would smile and look expectant, and actually enjoy it. Sometimes as time went on, he started to join in.

I'd change the chant too, so that he would not make the chant into a new script. Sometimes it would be the words or the rhythm or the pitch or the speed. It didn't matter which, but it made him sit up and notice. He started to actually interact with me and look for the exciting things I might do.

The improvements were slow, but they were there. Six months later and even still, four years later he still brings out his scripted language. But he doesn't repeat and repeat and repeat like he used to. Because his brain is processing so much better, he is more able to use his own speech and think for himself more often.

Our consultant recommended that each parent spend a dedicated half-hour per day with Cameron in a distraction-free room, working on our RDI objectives. The more we could do, the better it would be, but the half hour was a good start.

To be honest, I dreaded it. Even with coaching from the consultant, it was hard work coming up with a suitable activity that matched the learning objective, and it was hard work dealing with Cameron's desperate attempts to get out of having to think. Poor child. Learning dynamic thinking skills made him so anxious that every step of progress was like wading through thick mud.

The fact that we also videoed the sessions, analysed the clips and sent them in to be reviewed added stress to the whole exercise. I wanted to appear to be successful at what I was doing, but there were plenty of times when it was clear I had muffed the whole thing up and needed help. It was another lesson in humility.

Of course, the consultant never sat in judgment over us. She genuinely wanted to help us by seeing where we were at and offering useful suggestions. But I wasn't used to being incompetent, so I battled my own feelings of failure for a very long time.

Our progress started out, and continued to be cyclical, all the way along. I would begin keen and determined, ready to work with Cameron really well, and see lots of progress. A few bad days would see me get a little discouraged and lose a bit of momentum and I would give up for a while. Then I'd re-read some RDI material, or look back at my blog and see some progress, get re-inspired, and begin again, keen and determined... But for all the steps backward, there were so many forward steps that I decided I would never give up working with my beautiful son.

When he was still three, he had never asked a question beginning with the word 'Why', and he looked completely blank if we asked him one. Just before his fourth birthday, I was sitting in the lounge room one night when he came up to me and said, "Shirt off please mum."

Without thinking I said, "Why?" and started to help him take it off. Twenty seconds later he came back with the answer to the question, "wet". It was true—the sleeve was a little bit damp.

At six, I couldn't get him to stop asking 'why' questions because his ability to think and process had increased so much.

Again, just before the age of four, Cameron had a conversation with his grandma about his upcoming birthday. I wrote this down because I thought he had made such incredible progress in six months both in language and in engaging with people, despite the unusual ending of the exchange.

Grandma: "How old will you be on your birthday?"

Him: "Cameron is birthday cake."

Grandma: "Yes, you'll have a birthday cake. Yummy. But how many candles will you have on the cake?"

Him: "Birthday cake has candles."

Grandma: "You'll have four candles on your cake. You'll be four."

Him: "Cameron three."

Grandma: "Yes, soon you'll be four. You'll have your birthday and you'll be four."

Him: "Soon four. Cameron's birthday."

Grandma: "It will be Jasmine's birthday too. How old will she be?"

Him: "Not Jasmine's birthday. Cameron's birthday."

Grandma: "First yours, then sister's birthday. How many

candles will she have on her cake?"

Him: "Traffic lights."

Of course, I looked at this conversation even a year later and laughed. His thinking had become so much more sophisticated and his conversational skills were so much more advanced.

The hard work we were doing with him was paying off, even if the results were slow and steady, and even if I still found it easy to get a bit depressed about him the rest of the week.

I wrote on my blog: "Even with all his improvements, he's still a child on the autistic spectrum and I still have to fight him to go in and out the door, and work really hard in his RDI therapy. Life isn't normal, no matter how well he's doing."

Again, it was the people who saw him weekly or monthly who told me about the improvements they saw. The preschool teachers were especially good to talk to. It gave me a little shot of optimism in my week to hear that he had been happy, that he had done a painting or played happily or sat through the group time quietly. I truly appreciated them and the fact that I could 'share' him with other people who were enthusiastic about him.

* * *

What will life be like for ASD children when they grow up?

International research shows that outcomes for adults with autism are mixed. Many report lower rates of social inclusion and employment. They may have poor daily-living skills, and poor mental and physical health.

Individuals with higher IQ and better language skills have better outcomes, but around half of adults with autism remain living at home. Few marry, few have friends and less than half have any form of employment or education. Autistic adults report significantly lower quality of life than other people.

Making the transition out of secondary education is hard for adults with autism and family support is very important.

Data from the Australian Bureau of Statistics in 2014 shows that adults with autism have the lowest level of employment of any disability type, and this is echoed internationally. Many are underemployed or in part-time work. Successful outcomes may be found in supported programs, however.

Individuals with autism (and especially adults who receive a diagnosis later in life) are at high risk for other mental health conditions, most commonly anxiety and depression. They are also more at risk for medical conditions, including allergy, cardiovascular disease, obesity, neurologic disorders, gastrointestinal disorders and conditions associated with nutrition, as well as sleep difficulties.

Read more at www.psychology.org.au/inpsych/2017/april/richdale

10

Sticking together through it all

Another ongoing lesson in love that God had to teach me was with my husband.

At the time of Cameron's diagnosis, I felt like everything had stopped. But family life kept on going. I still had an eight month-old baby to feed and care for, a seven year-old daughter to play with, a dog to feed and walk, a house to clean and a husband to talk to. There was no 'pause' button I could press while I got the biggest problem of my life sorted out. Meals had to be cooked, homework had to be done, baths had to be taken.

I felt intensely stressed. I felt like I had to find help *now* for Cameron. If I didn't, he would lose precious time and I might lose him deeper into the autism. Unfortunately, it felt like there just wasn't enough time in the day to look after everything I had to do *and* search for help for him.

I was constantly anxious. I was tired, stressed and angry. I felt as though God had dropped me into the middle of a mud pit and was taking an awfully long time to get a rope to winch me out. I felt emotionally stretched beyond repair and the stress was so great that I developed an involuntary twitch in my top lip which quivered whenever I talked to people about how I was feeling. It felt like that funny little movement when you're about to cry but you're trying to hold it in. It made me feel vulnerable and out of control.

For a few months I felt as if I was operating on two planes. Normal life was relegated to automatic and all my conscious energy was directed to finding a therapy for Cameron that worked.

It caused problems with my relationship with my husband. Andrew was concerned about Cameron, but he didn't appear, at least outwardly, to be angry about the autism, or desperate like I was. Instead he felt hurt that I hardly spoke to him while I spent all my time on our son's needs.

I in turn was angry with him. Couldn't he see that our son's quality of life was at stake? Didn't he care enough to do what he could for him? Was he content to sit by and see our beautiful boy disintegrate more and more?

I wrote some harsh words in my diary at the time.

"Honestly, he does nothing about Cameron and then complains he doesn't feel loved or is supplanted by him. His son has autism! I'm so mad at him. If he wanted to 'feel loved' he could come and join in and help me."

It's just as well that at the same time as researching autism, I had also come across research on its effect on families. Divorce statistics for parents of a child with a disability are through the roof. Some people say that more than 80 percent of couples split up because of the stress of living with the disability and all that it entails.

I knew that I was grieving deep and hard. I also knew that grief affects people in different ways. I had an activist's grief. I have always been a 'doer' and finding solutions is my way to cope. My husband does things differently. I realised that if I continued to ignore him, we could fall apart. We had to stop, sit down and talk about what we were facing and feeling.

The year before had been a watershed in our marriage. We had addressed hidden issues that had hampered us for years. It had been painful as we both grappled with the truth of how flawed we were, but we had made an agreement then to tell the truth to each other, no matter what.

"I'm so angry with you," I managed to say one night, crying. "Do you even care? Can't you see that I need to do this to find something that will help him? I've got to do it now, otherwise it might be too late."

"I just see you killing yourself," he told me. "Of course I care about him. But we all live here. We all need things. If we only focus on Cameron, what happens to the other kids? And I miss you too."

"I'm killing myself doing this because no-one else is going to. I'm the mother. This is my child," I practically screamed. "Who else has his best interests at heart? Who else is going to fight for him? You've seen how useless the doctor's advice was. I've got to find something, soon, or what kind of life are we all going to have? Who else is going to love him if I don't love him enough to help him?"

"Please. Help me do this," I said. "Then I can come back and be normal again."

After hours of back and forth, with the usual accusations, defences, angry silences and tears that we always go through, and then with understanding and forgiveness, we found our middle point. He realised that we had to do this together, and I realised that I needed to go a little more gently.

We both knew from this point that facing Cameron's disability would be a huge test for us. We would just have to pull together, tell the truth and make a conscious decision to love each other no matter what. We vowed together that we wouldn't become part of the statistics and let this pull us apart. We knew our children all needed us, and that God would give us the strength to cope somehow. The years that followed were not easy, but we knew that we were committed to sticking it out, even when it got really tough.

It was not until several years later that I realized why we had reacted so differently. In fact, it's normal—and it's because of the 'internal emotional system' that every couple or partnership has.

The first time I ever saw this at work for myself was on a trip to Europe that I took with a friend, straight out of school.

My friend and I had been travelling for about two months already and our differences were clearly evident. She loved museums; I preferred to walk down main streets and in parks. She wanted to talk to other tourists; I preferred my own space with a book. She was generally calm, laissez-faire and easygoing; I was the one who panicked and worried about whether we'd miss planes or trains or buses.

For some reason, in Czechoslovakia, we just couldn't find our way around the buses and trains. On our second evening after a full day of sightseeing we worked very hard to get on what we believed was the correct train. But after 20 minutes of travel, it seemed we were not heading in any recognisable direction.

"We'll have to get out and wait for one coming the other way," said my friend, so we hopped out at the next stop.

The station was completely deserted. It looked and felt like the middle of nowhere. We sat under the one, solitary yellow light at the end of the platform, hugging our summer weight jackets around ourselves, hoping that a return train would come soon to take us back.

It sounds scary, and at any other time, I would have been terrified, but this time I was elated. Somehow, the thought that we were completely out of control and there was nothing I could do about it was freeing. I sat and felt the edges of the night breeze on my face.

My friend, on the other hand, was, unusually for her, completely out of her mind with worry, panic and fear. She paced and pounded and talked to herself while I relaxed and enjoyed the experience. It was as if we had swapped personalities for the night.

Afterwards I wondered about it. Why wasn't I worried or upset about being stuck in the middle of nowhere? The difference was that this time, my friend started to worry first. Because she was carrying the worry burden, I didn't have to. I was free to enjoy the experience, knowing that enough worry was being done already. I think I knew instinctively that if I was terrified too, we would both spiral into a pit of fear and neither of us would be able to function.

Every couple or partnership has a similar kind of emotional balancing act or pressure gauge. It's rare for both people to be really excited or very depressed at the same time. If one is low, the other one holds it together for them both. If one is high, the other will stay a little bit more grounded.

When Andrew and I learned that Cameron had autism, I was the one who fell immediately into panic mode. I was the one scrabbling around for answers, going on crying jags and seeing only despair and worst case scenarios for the future. I was immediately depressed and constantly worried as well as being emotionally fatigued and physically exhausted on a daily basis, just from having to deal with his behaviour. I saw not only a hard and unhappy life ahead for him, but also for me, as his primary care-giver.

With me feeling so much negative emotion, it was impossible for him to feel the same way. If he, too, had gone down to the depths, who would have been there to pull us both out? Instead, he buried a lot of his fear, anger and sorrow so that we both wouldn't go under.

The delicate balancing act that we were unconsciously playing out had its own repercussions. I felt resentful and angry when I saw what looked to me like him just staying out of it, and leaving everything to me.

"Great," I would mutter to myself. "As if life's not hard enough, now I'm the one who's going to have to deal with this, because I'm the only one who cares."

At the same time, he felt pressured to hold me up and not crumble while it seemed that I was going to pieces.

Even though we knew we had to manage under all the pressure, the topic of autism became a hot button in our relationship. To him, it seemed like I wanted to talk about it constantly and would push him to participate. To me, it seemed that he never wanted to talk about it and would make every excuse to get out of the conversation. I felt unsupported by him. He felt weighed down by me.

It didn't help that in the year after diagnosis, when we were starting out with our therapy and dealing with perhaps the worst behaviour we had experienced yet from Cameron, Andrew was also: looking for a job, finding a job, finishing his final exams from a punishing four-year course, packing to move to a new town, finding his way around the new area, starting a completely new job in a whole new career, doing many things for the first time ever as part of his job (including weddings and funerals which take a high level of emotional energy) and meeting hundreds of new people, all of whom expected friendliness, compassion, competence and boundless wisdom of him.

"I have to support my family," was his underlying worry. "I need to succeed at this because they're all depending on me."

I wanted him home more, but he couldn't be home more, and that became an issue as well. He felt pressured as he was pulled in every direction. I felt pressured as I took the responsibility for the three children, dealt with Cameron's tantrums and managed the therapy.

Every day for a long period was tense, tight and highly explosive. We just had to keep going and look after ourselves as individuals as much as we could so that our relationship as a couple wouldn't self-destruct.

I tried to learn to be less 'needy' and find other ways to get the support and love I needed—because Andrew just couldn't give me everything I needed. He tried to learn to step up and give more, even when all he wanted was to be on his own.

A couple of times a year my mother would offer to have Cameron for a weekend at her place, or to babysit all three children while Andrew and I went out shopping or for a movie. The feeling of weight being taken off in those times was unbelievable. We got to feel a little bit like we did when things were easier, and we were grateful.

Unfortunately, though, it meant that coming back to the same situation was almost more unbearable. When a heavy weight is lifted, the relief is immense. But when the weight goes back on, it feels twice as heavy while you get used to it again. I would find that not only would I have to 'recover' from time out, but Cameron would also have bad days while he recovered from the change, and I wondered if it was even worthwhile taking breaks. If we didn't know how good things could be, surely we wouldn't miss it?

We managed to survive by developing techniques for communication that were more effective in less time (we simply didn't have the time we wanted to hash everything out), by setting boundaries around our conversations about both work and therapy, and by acknowledging that neither of us could meet all the other person's needs. We tried not to take things personally and learned to look at the real reasons we felt bad, rather than blaming each other.

To continue under intensely high pressure circumstances is incredibly difficult. I'm in awe of couples who not only stay together, but also stay friends when life is chronically, persistently hard. Thankfully for us, the pressure began to be lifted as Cameron's therapy began to work.

* * *

In my humble opinion… how much can you cope with?

I always try to remember that people just want to be helpful when they talk to me about autism, but I still get surprised with some of the things that come out.

I've had this phrase said to me a number of times: "Well, God doesn't give you what you can't cope with." And every time, I have wanted to say, "Yes, he darn well does, thank you very much."

Unfortunately, while on one level it may be true that 'God doesn't give you what you can't cope with', it doesn't help to say it. If God gave my child autism because he thought I could cope, then there must have been something seriously wrong with me because for years I didn't think I was coping at all!

I'm of the opinion that God doesn't expect us to 'cope' on our own. Not only will he help us when we reach the end of ourselves, but he's put us in a Body of believers. The whole body is meant to care and support a part of itself that isn't 'coping'.

God does give us what we can't cope with because he knows that we grow in him as we ask for help and we grow in the body more as we ask for and give support.

11

God, grant me patience. And hurry!

The concept of patience has always intrigued me. I never really understood what it meant to be patient or to have patience. I knew what 'putting up with something' was and I could do it fairly well for a while, pasting on a smile or a cool demeanour, but I was always cranky afterwards.

The early years of having children even without the complication of autism had shown me just how impatient I was. I could see how getting more patience would improve both my life and the lives of my children. I really wanted to change and I had had many discussions with my friends about how I could get patience, and what it would look like.

After a while, I thought, 'well, it's listed as a fruit of the Spirit in the Bible, so God can give it to me,' and I began to pray earnestly and eagerly, "Lord, give me patience."

As they say, you've got to be careful what you pray for.

And as my mother always said, "If you want to learn patience, you've got to have something to be patient about."

I knew that I would be given something—a challenge—to help me to grow patience, but I didn't realise just how much patience would be required, and how much suffering would be needed for it to grow.

The challenge came in the form of Cameron's meltdowns

Our Sunday mornings were always difficult, and often seemed to spark off a meltdown. One particular morning was an absolute nightmare. Andrew had already left the house for the early church service. He wouldn't be back for hours, and it was my job to get everyone to church for the next service. Unfortunately, I overslept and then made the children scoff their cereal while I quickly had a shower and found some half-decent clothes for myself. When I emerged dripping from the bathroom, I heard Cameron yelling at the other end of the house,

"No church! Noooooo Church! Church is bad. Noooooo!"

Just great.

I didn't know what had happened to set him off, but after fifteen minutes of screaming and protesting, it was clear that there was no way that he was going to come quietly.

I examined my options.

The obvious was to give in. But that wasn't really an option. We all go to church. It's pretty much a non-negotiable in our house. Besides, it wasn't fair to deprive Jasmine of her time with friends at Kids Church. We all just had to go.

The second option was to ring for help. Unfortunately, this one wasn't really an option either. Andrew was busy organising for the service and no-one else except me could handle Cameron. I suppose someone else could have taken the other children and I could have stayed with him at home, but that wasn't really an option either because of the first reason. Plus, I hated to impose on other people; I felt that once I started doing that, it might never stop.

The third option was to wait until he calmed down and then go. It was a possibility, except that I had also thought of the fourth option, which was to take him anyway and count on him calming down once we were there.

I decided that the fourth was the best option. I knew that it could take up to half an hour to calm him, either here or there, but I knew that if I tried to move him again having calmed him here, he could very easily explode again, so calming there was the better option.

So, with a cranky face, and not a few choice words going in my head I snipped at the other two children to "get ready to go NOW!", packed bags and snacks, and loaded the car with everything we needed, having decided that our usual walk would be impossible.

I then walked into the office, where I confronted my screaming boy, picked him up kicking and squirming, manhandled him out of the house and plopped him in the car in the seat next to the door with the child locks. They are useful things, child locks.

When we got to church, I pulled right up next to the door and let Jasmine out so she could join her friends. And then I just sat in the car with the boys and waited.

After about ten minutes of screaming, Cameron let me cuddle him. Then it took another ten minutes of huffing and puffing to talk about putting shoes on and then another five minutes to think up creative ways to get out of the car without it seeming like we were getting out of the car.

We got to church. We even got in the door. But I was a complete and utter mess for the rest of the day and could hardly talk to anyone. How was I ever going to manage more days like this one? Could I possibly ever be patient enough to not let it get to me?

Meltdowns are a special feature of daily life with a child who has ASD. From the age of two and a half to about four, Cameron had, on average, six or seven major meltdowns per day. They involved kicking, screaming, head banging, running through the house, throwing things around and other generally uncontrollable and extremely undesirable behaviour.

A number of times, I tried to explain to people around me how difficult I found it dealing with the constant outbursts. I'd be greeted by knowing looks from parents of other small children.

"Oh, yes," they would say. "Just the other day my Jack threw one in the supermarket. Soooo embarrassing!"

The implication was that there was nothing different about my child, because every child throws tantrums. They are normal.

And that is true—to a degree. I had already experienced them with Jasmine, who had been an expert at the pinching, hitting and hair pulling kind from the age of two. At the age of three she wrote 'No Mummy' on the wall when something didn't go her way. (It was in black permanent texta, but that's another story.) Up to the age of five she was having regular screaming matches with me when she got overtired which, unfortunately, happened a lot.

But there *are* differences with ASD meltdowns. One of the differences is that they are almost completely unpredictable. I could usually understand why my daughter threw her wobblies, but I could hardly ever pinpoint the exact reasons why Cameron exploded.

One morning, when he was three and a half, we had just come back inside the house. Cameron sat down, took two shoes and one sock off, and then began crying. He yelled for his sister and dad who were out at her hockey game and then screamed, "Max's room, Max's room," at the top of his lungs. At that point he ran sobbing to Max's bedroom where he climbed into the cot and continued to cry for the next half hour.

I had no idea what had happened and I still can't even try to guess at it.

The other difference with ASD tantrums is that it is almost impossible to talk or reason the child out of it. Cameron learned that he could use words to express his anxieties at the age of six . Back when he was smaller, with much poorer understanding, it was useless to say what I would have said to my daughter at the same age, which was something like, "Hey honey, next time you're sad, you can use words to say how you feel."

I think ASD meltdowns are like the tantrums of a 12 to 18 month-old in that you're dealing with pure emotions that are completely out of the child's control. You are also dealing with a child who is constantly anxious and overwhelmed—much more so than with other children.

I once heard an adult with autism say, "I still feel like I'm constantly on the edge, on the precipice of everything," and I realised that when Cameron was young, his tantrums were his reaction to falling off the edge.

With many children you can often head the meltdown off at the pass, but with a child with ASD, there's only a tiny window for bringing calm back to the situation. With most children, you can often talk about the meltdown once everyone is recovered. With children with ASD, it's very difficult to revisit anxious feelings. With the majority of children, you know that tantrums are part of a stage that every child will go through and will almost always be over by the age of five. With a child with ASD you don't know when, if ever, it will stop.

A lot of Cameron's meltdowns took place in shops and parks. Ashamed as I am to say it, most of my worry was about what other people would think of me as a mother when he screamed, ran away and generally appeared disobedient and obstreperous.

The first time I was criticised in public was just before his diagnosis. We were on holidays in Queensland and I had been taking him in the stroller every day to the local shop to buy food for dinner. Once or twice I had bought a lollipop at the same time and on this particular day he wanted another one.

"Lollipop, lollipop, lollipop," he shouted at the top of his voice, as we stood in the queue waiting to pay.

"No lollipop today. Just going home," said I, trying to appear calm, and desperately wishing the people in front of me had bought fewer groceries so we could get out quicker.

It took less than a minute for him to escalate to a full-blown meltdown with kicking legs, waving arms, red face and screams and shouts of, "lolllllipop! lolllllipop!"

I stood at the counter for about three minutes enduring the noise and secretly wishing the floor would swallow me. Finally, the people in front paid and left and it was my turn to check out. Cameron was still screaming as I packed the last of the groceries into the stroller, but he stopped long enough for me to hear an elderly man behind me make a comment to the person next to him.

"When my kids were little they were brought up on the end of a strap," he said with pure disdain in his voice. "They would never have even thought to make a fuss like that."

I felt my blood pressure go up in a second—as if it wasn't high enough already. And to my shame, I turned to him and said, "Well. I'll bet your wife did most of the work with your children anyway!" before storming out the door with my shopping.

Another public meltdown came at the local pool. Cameron always loved to swim, and it was nice to have a source of happiness that I could rely on. The prospect of guaranteed joy for all three children for a few hours made me willing to gamble on what would happen once we were ready to get out of the water and go home.

On this particular day we had had a great swim, and Cameron had gotten out easily for once. We headed to the dressing rooms, and as we got dressed I popped a white T-shirt over his head. Silly me. I thought he might not notice that it wasn't one of his favourite shirts.

He noticed.

"Shirt off, Shirt off!" he howled.

'No, I'll persist. He has to learn and these people around me will think I'm a pushover parent if I can't control him,' I thought to myself and I kept the shirt on.

He howled louder, the women in the change-room started staring and my cheeks turned red. After a two minute struggle, Cameron tore all his clothes completely off and ran, completely naked, out the door and through the pool complex like a demented little soul, with me running after him and my poor mother bringing up the rear with the other two (dressed) children behind.

Church also saw its fair share of explosions. One day, for some reason, Cameron had it in his head that he wanted to go home in the red car but I was determined that we would walk home.

The trip home was noisy with him screaming, "Red Car Red Car Red Car." In the end it became violent. He dropped to the pavement and banged his head on the concrete. I picked him up, concerned that he might hurt himself, but he was too strong for me and threw himself in a nearby rosebush once I put him down.

Our very gracious and elegant neighbour came out to see what the trouble was and helpfully wheeled the pram with the baby for me while I wrestled Cameron home and inside the door. It took 20 minutes to make a five minute walk home.

The public meltdowns were distressing and embarrassing

and overwhelming for me as well as Cameron. I found it slightly easier to deal with the inside ones, only because the embarrassment factor wasn't there. These were blowups that we faced all the time. They happened when we tried to get Cameron to; make transitions from play to meal time; sit at the table; eat new food; eat any regular food; have breakfast; go to the toilet; go out to play; come in from play; go up the steps (as opposed to the path) at his sister's school; get in the bath; get out of the bath, and so on and so forth.

Dealing with the constant screaming and yelling was never easy. There were times when I swore, usually but not always under my breath. There were times when I put my head down on the kitchen bench and cried, wishing that it would all go away. There were times when I yelled back or snapped at the other children or marched away and slammed my door.

But there were also times when even though I thought I couldn't go on any longer, or do it anymore, that I realised that I loved this child, and if I wasn't going to help him, then no-one would. It was out of sheer, desperate necessity that I could somehow find another scrap of energy—from either me or from God somehow—to quiet my own angry heart and offer my son the calmness that he needed so much.

I had prayed for patience, and knew that I would get a challenge, but it was a lot bigger than I imagined it would be. These tantrums were the things that were going to grow the patience I had hungered after.

And amazingly, somehow, it worked. The meltdowns taught me to be patient through unpredictability, through noise, through public humiliation, through being constantly overwhelmed and through not knowing when it all might end.

Patience is part of love. When I focused on loving my child

instead of meeting my own desires for social acceptability, I became a lot more patient.

I am still nowhere near as patient as I want to be, but I have more of it now than I ever did. I find that there are fewer things that stress me out now. I have a greater ability to give time and understanding to people. I'm not perfect, but I'm better than I was. God answered my prayer, even though I wouldn't have chosen the pain that went with it. You don't get patience by having an easy, stress-free life!

But patience was just one part of dealing with the meltdowns. The other part came in learning how to help my boy find peace and calm, how to deal with my own preconceived ideas about being a good parent, and how to help stop us both from falling off the edge all the time.

* * *

In my humble opinion… Why do we avoid people who are a little bit different?

To answer that it helps to understand the concept of regulation. Regulation is the give and take, the pull and push, the back and forth that is required to make a social exchange.

You could think of it in terms of playing tennis. Two people stand on opposite ends of the court. They hit the ball back and forth. To make it a game worth playing, they should both be able to hit back and forth pretty evenly. They must be able to regulate to each other's ability.

Having a conversation with someone (adult or child) who cannot regulate adequately is kind of like me playing tennis with Venus Williams. I can't hit quick shots. I can't serve decently. For our interaction to even be called 'tennis', Venus would have to change her game seriously and bring it down to my level. And quite honestly, she probably wouldn't want to play like that.

There are always at least two players in any conversation or social exchange. But if one player keeps dropping the ball, or doesn't get what's going on, the others must take on more responsibility to make sure the exchange doesn't fail.

If you take on more responsibility in the exchange, you are 'regulating' for the other person.

Regulating is not relaxing or easy. It's quite hard to change the way you naturally relate to others. The more you have to regulate when you don't expect to have to regulate, the less comfortable the encounter or friendship.

So if a person looks like she should be able to relate on a peer level, but you find that it's not quite working and you have to change your game, it becomes awkward and difficult. More often than not, we leave or avoid the person and never go back.

12

Taming the meltdown triggers

Sometimes love means learning more, changing things you hold dear and letting go of what you've always done. I had to do a lot of changing and letting go as I learned how to help my boy calm down and get rid of his tantrums.

Unlike some parts of Australia, it was really cold in winter where we lived. The wind blew through you if you didn't dress right. You needed all the gloves, scarves, beanies and jackets you could get.

Cameron hated the wind and the cold, but he also refused point blank to wear his winter jacket. Every effort that I made to get him to wear it turned into a meltdown on his part, but I just didn't feel I was being a good mother unless I had tried to get it on him.

One cold afternoon, I had to walk my daughter and her two friends down the street to their after-school club, near the library. I decided that today was the day Cameron would wear his jacket.

It didn't work.

Picture me with a baby in a pram plus three other children and a bag of library books getting out the door with Cameron yelling at the top of his lungs, "Jacket Off Jacket Off Jacket Off!"

He wouldn't walk, and I couldn't leave him at home on his own, so I carried him under one arm kicking and screaming, whilst pushing the pram with the other arm, across two roads and up to the Kids' Club hall.

The little girls were very helpful but slightly overawed by the fracas. I sent them in while Cameron, with his jacket now off, headed behind a large bush and melted down for a while. The baby and I waited until he calmed a little and decided, himself, to join the bigger children in the hall.

From that point, he was fine. We went to the library as normal. And the jacket stayed off.

The next bout of kicking and screaming was triggered by bath time...

I had to trust that in time, the diet changes and the RDI work we were doing with Cameron would help him process things better and live a calmer life. That was the aim anyway.

Until then, however, I had to learn a few things about how to handle him, myself and the triggers for the tantrums.

For a long time, I couldn't see that I brought a lot of meltdowns on myself. I would be determined that he should wear the shirt/eat the food/do the thing I had chosen, and it became a battle of wills, which I lost, time after time.

My attitude was, 'well, he's being naughty, he has to learn, and if it takes tantrums to learn, so be it.'

I didn't realise that a lot of the time he was actually incapable of processing what I wanted him to do, and the reason why I wanted him to do it. Nor did I realise that he resisted whenever he felt incompetent or uncertain. His brain had not made enough connections to do the thing I wanted him to do and he had no other way to express it. He wasn't being naughty—he just plain couldn't do it.

I didn't realise that every time he had a meltdown, he learned less and increased his anxious feelings. I didn't realise that he couldn't possibly learn anything while he was in such a crazy state.

Then I found the book *The Explosive Child* by Ross Greene which changed a lot of my thinking.

The first thing that had to change was my belief about having to 'win' the battle of wills and instead, focus on helping him to learn to calm himself down and cope with uncertainty. So far, he hadn't learned a thing in all the tantrums that he'd been having. What I'd been doing obviously wasn't working, so I needed to change my approach.

I began to see his meltdowns as a struggle against his own difficult life rather than a struggle against me. It made it easier to find better solutions when I wasn't personally involved.

The next thing that had to change was getting rid of tantrum triggers. The old parenting advice says 'pick your battles' because really, there are a lot of things that just aren't worth worrying about.

Greene described it nicely as a 'three basket' approach.

Basket A is for the things you must insist on. These are things which are truly necessary or else the child will die or self-harm. For example, you must enforce that the child shall stay beside you when near a busy road.

Basket B is for the things that you would like to happen. These things are important right now and things that the child is able to cope with.

Basket C is for the things that you are not going to bother about yet. These are things that are not important right now. If you have a battle of wills and a meltdown over these things, it is a waste of everyone's time and energy.

I sat back and looked at the things I was expecting of Cameron every day. Were they essential to life and safety? For the most part, no. It was easy enough to put a few basics into Basket A, like road safety, not playing with knives, and staying away from matches.

Basket B was trickier. I knew that I had high standards for my children. I liked them to be nicely dressed, clean and brushed, well-behaved, able to sit still at dinner and happy to eat what I gave them. I wanted them to be polite to their relatives and older friends, say hello and goodbye and answer questions with confidence and respect. I wanted them to come when I called, do what I asked, and go to bed at 7pm sharp.

In the past, most of these had been in my Basket A. I could see now that none of them were essential to life or safety, but I desperately wanted all them to at least be in basket B. However, I also knew that the daily tantrums over clothes and food and the nightly tantrums over dinner and bath time were not working out for us.

It killed me to throw some of these things into basket C. But after some hard thinking, in the end, I came to the conclusion that I wanted these things for myself. If I had nice, clean, smiling children who jumped on command, I would be seen as a good mother, a successful homemaker, and a nice, spiritual Christian.

I had to ask myself, was I more concerned about my own reputation, or was I going to do what was best for my son who was having so much trouble every day? Love meant I had to give up my own self-serving expectations.

I dumped a whole lot of things into the third basket. Clothes and shoes were a big one to go. What he wore and who chose it were really unimportant in the grand scheme of life. I put the nice buttoned shirts and the tailored trousers away for his little brother and went with his standard uniform of crocs, track pants and long sleeved t-shirts, night and day, summer and winter, in bold solid colours only. I looked back at the swimming pool tantrum over the white, short-sleeved t-shirt and shook my head in disbelief. I couldn't believe I did that to him, or myself. The agony just wasn't worth it.

Also into basket C went a whole lot of food issues. Again, it wasn't worth killing myself over making him eat new food. I presented him with the same balanced, albeit boring, meal every night and hoped it would get eaten. If he protested against his gluten-free bread, I brought out GF crackers. If crackers were unpopular, I replaced them with whatever it was he wanted that was ok for him to eat. I just didn't want to ruin everyone's meal time because he was screaming, night after night.

Things like which door he used to get in and out of the car, how many buttons he pressed on the dashboard on the way out, and the route he took to get into the house also went into Basket C, along with chores such as cleaning up his room and making his bed which he obviously couldn't handle.

To my own public embarrassment, I also decided that I wouldn't push him to answer other people's too-difficult questions, or expect that he would sit up for meals at other people's houses. I simply said, "he won't be eating with us," and brought toys or a video for him to entertain himself with.

Pyjamas, regular baths and well-brushed hair also disappeared into Basket C. It was liberating for me to not have to fight the nightly battles. If he was really filthy, I'd bring in a warm washcloth and get rid of the dirt gently that way.

Over time, things have moved from Basket C to Basket B, but at the beginning, I made sure we only had a few things in there, including wearing a hat at preschool, saying please, thank you, hello and goodbye to people and answering my simple questions.

It was a good start. The numbers of tantrums did reduce, and Cameron became calmer and happier for longer periods of the day.

That took care of the triggers.

But what about the next part? We couldn't just reduce the stress in Cameron's life and expect things to be like that forever, could we? Surely he'd have to learn somehow, sometime to process things, to think more flexibly and to be able to control his outbursts.

To begin with, the changes came from me. I learned to slow down, to take more time and to keep myself calm. I learned not to panic when he lost it and melted down. I began to learn if his protest was a serious one, or if I could just ignore it and continue on. And of course, I learned that my worth didn't come from looking like a 'successful' parent.

Our half hour per day of focused 'guiding' also helped Cameron to make more connections in his brain which enabled him to cope with more change. He became, gradually and bit by bit, more flexible. He began to learn to calm himself down.

From the beginning, he had never been able to cope with too many words and too much language, so turning off my mouth was a big help. It also helped to wind back the demands I was making of him if I could see he wasn't coping.

We saw improvements quite quickly after making the changes, but it went in a 'two steps forward, one step back' kind of pattern. We would have a few calm weeks followed by a number of uptight episodes, and then it would all start over again. I tried to keep a log of them in my blog, and included the things I did that made it better or worse.

Today was another of 'those days', where Cameron just couldn't cope with anything. He tantrumed to turn off the TV, get in the car, go into the shops. He tantrumed at lunch, dinner and bath, and then again at bed. It was all too much.

So when it came time for RDI, I decided to play it cool and take it very easy. I hardly used any words at all, and concentrated on physical co-regulation. We rocked a lot of the time, him sitting on my lap. We moved front and back, and then side to side, and then when I thought he was calm enough, we circled around together.

I tried to play a finger game with him at one point early on, but he couldn't cope with the interaction so we went to a row-row-your boat action which was easier for him.

By the end he was well regulated and was able to cope with a 'falling in the mud and cleaning up' game with me, but in general, everything I did was all very slow, quiet and rhythmic.

I seem to be getting better at calming him down when he really throws a wobbly. I hold him on my lap and just rock back and forward gently. After ten minutes, or when I judge he's peaceful enough, I make a comment on something we can both see, or something about him, for example, "There's a bird in the garden," or "You've got ten toes on your feet."

I don't offer questions or abstract ideas as he seems to calm quicker if he focuses on something concrete.

As his language and brain connections improved, I found that humour helped defuse some situations. One day, when Cameron yelled "I won't!" at me, I yelled back in just the same tone, but with a smile on my face. He looked surprised and then stopped.

"You sound like a huge lion when you do that!" I said, and, "You sound like an angry hippopotamus." It got a smile and headed off the meltdown.

I was also able to start helping him to think ahead to potentially difficult situations.

After a particularly bad Sunday morning one week, I whispered into Cameron's ears on the next Saturday night, "We're going to church tomorrow. No crying for church, ok?"

He looked up at me and said, "No crying for church. Church is smile!" And he did.

It took a good two years of participating in the RDI Program, together with diet changes and homeopathy to get our daily lives mostly calm and liveable. It was a good three and a half years before I could say that we were generally tantrum-free. In the meantime, we all developed tougher skin and thicker ear-drums. We had to have more of a sense of humour, and we all, father, mother, sister and brother, had to learn to keep calm even when we felt like screaming too.

That turned out to be pretty hard for his siblings. They also had lessons in patience and slowing down which will be with them for life.

13

Siblings, loyalty and rivalry

Loving one child as God loves them is challenging and stretching and takes everything you have. Loving three? Well, I knew I definitely needed divine help for that.

From the very beginning, Cameron and his big sister Jasmine were good friends. He adored her, and being almost exactly four years older than he, she enjoyed helping me to look after him. When he was able to walk she began to organise his playtimes and he followed along with eager obedience. It was a delight to watch them race around the lounge room playing chase, being lions and making cubby houses together, under her direction of course.

As he got older, Jasmine began to notice that he was not talking as well as other children. She could also see the difficulties I was having in managing his behaviour. She was confused, but also fiercely protective of him. Many times she did better than I did in calming him down, handling his tantrums, or working out what he wanted. If Andrew or I lost our temper with him, she would be furious with us.

Jasmine was six when we began Cameron's journey of diagnosis. Once things became serious, I realised we had a choice. We could keep her in the dark and never talk about autism or what

Cameron's difficulties were, or we could tell her what was going on.

We chose to tell her. We had always had a close relationship and as a bright and articulate child with her own opinions, she had always been part of our discussions. It was obvious that she could see that Cameron was different from the children around them, and I thought it would be frustrating for her to not know the reason.

I was also confident that she wouldn't use the information against him. Perhaps if she had been younger, she might have used his difference to tease or torment him, but that was never the case.

Trying to figure out how to tell a six year old about autism was a bit tricky especially when at the beginning, I hardly understood it myself.

"Cameron has something called autism," I explained to her. "He's not sick, and he's not going to die. What it means is that his brain works a bit differently from most people. So that's why he's having trouble talking. And that's probably why he gets angry a lot."

"Will he get better?" she asked.

"I hope so. But it will probably take a long time. So Daddy and I will be learning about it and trying to find something that is going to help him. And of course, we'll be praying for God to help him get better too."

Cameron's unusual behaviours were very apparent to Jasmine's friends, who often came over to play, and giggled nervously when he repeated the ends of their words or ran yelling and screaming from the table.

I was pleased that Jasmine had something to tell them, although I don't know how difficult it might have been for her to do it.

One day I heard her telling her six year-old friend, "His brain works a little bit differently, which is why he can't quite speak right. We have to teach him things so he'll know what to do."

The friend still appeared nonplussed by some of Cameron's antics, but seemed to accept him a little bit better.

I was very aware that a large part of my energy was being directed towards Cameron's therapies and appointments. An even larger part was used up just managing the day to day difficulties of living with a child with ASD and ADHD. I was grieving, sad and often angry. There wasn't much energy left to give to anyone, let alone Jasmine or the baby.

From what I had read, however, I knew that I needed to give Jasmine the space to express herself and live her own life. I didn't want her to take a second seat to her brother with special needs. I was terrified that she might become resentful of me, and angry with him. I was especially worried when, about the same time as his diagnosis, she developed a chronic cough and soon after that, a facial tic. Now, as well as dragging Cameron around to doctors, I was making appointments for Jasmine at the children's hospital, trying to find out if she had a serious respiratory problem!

I became convinced that the tic and cough were her unconscious reactions to the high levels of stress in our family. It made me more determined to not put her needs behind the other children.

Even though it hurt me to hear one of my children criticise the other, I tried hard to be open to talk about the difficulties of living with ASD with Jasmine if she needed to.

One day, during a trip to Sydney on the train, Jasmine and I endured the noise of Cameron and his baby brother both screaming at ear-splitting levels in unison for an entire half hour. Nothing I did could calm the chaos. After things had quietened down a little she said to me, "Mummy, I really hope I don't have a child like Cameron when I grow up."

My heart felt absolutely wrenched. But I took a deep breath and tried to look beyond the criticism. Really, I was glad that she felt she could express herself. She wasn't trying to be mean or rude. She just saw that I was struggling and realised that sometimes things are harder than you hope for.

"You know honey," I said to her, "nobody *wants* to have a child who has struggles. Of course not! But sometimes it happens. It's hard. We just have to love them even more and help them to get through it."

She considered a minute, and then said, "Mummy, if I have a baby with autism when I grow up, you'll know just what to do to help me."

I was glad she had so much confidence in me. I wasn't sure I had that much confidence in myself!

With all the children, it has been a challenge to ignore my automatic reaction of trying to shut them down when they get angry or frustrated with each other. Over time I became convinced of the importance of listening without judgement to their feelings, whether negative or positive. The theory is that if they 'feel heard', they become more able to deal with their own feelings and will grow up with better emotional health than if they are never allowed to express frustration or anger.

One day when Jasmine was about eight, I took her out to buy some new clothes. We walked around the department store, looking at everything. I fingered a navy blue dress with admiration.

"I like this one. What do you think?" I asked her.

"No. I don't like it at all," she said.

I thought it was cute, so I was a little bit disappointed. "What's wrong with it? Is it the style?" I asked.

"No. It's the colour. It reminds me of Cameron. I don't like it. I'm never going to wear it."

It was true. Navy blue was the colour of Cameron's favourite tops, pants and 'croc' shoes. He hardly ever wore anything else. I was disappointed, and it would have been easy for me to say, "Don't think that. Navy is lovely. There's nothing wrong with it, just because Cameron wears it. Anyway, why wouldn't you want to be like your brother? You love him, don't you?"

But every book I had read about children with special needs siblings talked about the way parents often denied their frustrations and annoyances and pretended they didn't exist. I was determined not to do it. I swallowed my annoyance and moved on to look at purple t-shirts and pink jeans.

Sometimes, after a difficult afternoon of tantrums or because of her own tiredness, Jasmine just couldn't cope with Cameron. Rather than have fights at the table, I often let go of my desire for us all to have a 'lovely family dinner' and instead let her eat in her room so that she wouldn't explode with frustration. In the car, I have frequently taken the uncomfortable place in the middle of the back seat rather than let children's tempers fray.

What we've learned in our family is that angry explosions of temper or shouting do absolutely nothing towards solving a problem of behaviour. Cameron just cannot cope with other people's intense emotions. What might have started as irritating behaviour or a small frustration between the children becomes ten times worse and lasts ten times as long if we parents yell or bang or crash, or if we let the kids get to a place where they yell, bang or crash. We *have* to keep our cool, and we *have* to head the difficulties off at the pass before they escalate and take over. And then, we have to let everyone simmer down and express how they feel.

Cameron's relationship with his sister was one thing. His relationship with his brother was a whole different ballgame.

Almost from the beginning they were rivals. And sadly, most of the jealousy was from Cameron's side to begin with. Max would wake up looking for his big brother and was excited to play with him—at least until the first head-butt, bite attempt or hair pull.

Of course, it's normal for children born two years apart to be rivals, and jealousy of a younger brother is certainly not new in the world, but I wondered if perhaps it was exacerbated by the ASD. My theory was that the baby represented uncertainty for Cameron and dealing with him may have required more flexibility than he was capable of.

For a long time I could not leave the two boys in the same room for more than a minute before I heard one of them yowl his head off. When I went in to keep the peace again, I would usually find Cameron holding the baby captive in a corner, or Max launching himself onto Cameron, mouth open wide, ready for a bite.

After a while, things improved. My joy was inexpressible the first time I heard them actually play together. I wanted to record their happy voices and keep them forever.

I began to give them every opportunity I could to improve their relationship. Over time I had become a lot more flexible in my parenting and was relatively unfussed about things like strict bedtimes. Because Cameron was still not able to get himself to sleep until 10 or 11pm, my only requirement was that they play quietly in their rooms until they felt sleepy.

One night I was tired, and watching TV with Andrew. Both boys were still awake and were supposed to be in their rooms, but had migrated to another part of the house.

I was annoyed. "I'd better go and put the boys to bed or put them back in their rooms," I said to my husband.

But from where he was sitting, he could see what was going on.

"Hang on," he said. "You should see the game they are playing together. They are actually relating really well and playing in a coordinated way."

I craned my head around the door to have a look and it was true. Somehow, after a day of hitting each other, they had reached a happy point and were running around together, getting into 'boats' and rescuing each other. It was real game. Each of them had a role, both were contributing to it, and both were having a fabulous time.

"Their relationship is more important than bedtime right now," I said to Andrew. "I'm going to take the bigger picture view. What they are both learning from this game is great stuff."

We left them for another 20 minutes and they didn't falter in their coordination once. When finally they'd had enough, they were more than ready to turn in to bed.

Since then, it's been 'best of friends, worst of enemies' for both boys. The good times are wonderful and the bad times are just what every other child with any sibling has ever experienced.

* * *

What's the future for siblings?

There's no conclusive study that points to either a 'positive' or 'negative' outcome for siblings of a child with autism. Like much of life, having a brother or sister with ASD brings with it benefits and downsides.

Of course, family communication and mindset has a lot to do with how children process and come to think about things. A 1986 study reported that siblings viewed their relationship with their sibling with autism more positively when they accepted the child's role as a member of the family, they perceived minimal parental favouritism and they were not worried about the future of the child with autism. Position in the family also made a difference. Children from larger families did better, as did those who were older than their sibling with autism, or where there was a large age difference between siblings.

Fact sheets:

- *www.timeforafuture.com.au/fact_sheets/sibling-issues.htm*
- https://www.autismspectrum.org.au/sites/default/files/Factsheet_Siblings_20170401.pdf

Article:

- *Autistic Kids—the Sibling Problem by Amy Lennard Goehner, 24 December 2007 in Time Magazine.* This is available on the internet and provides a good summary of common problems siblings face with some good solutions.

Website:

- *www.raisingchildren.net.au This site has a comprehensive, helpful section on helping siblings of autistic children.*

14

I'm still just so unhappy!

God had me on the path of learning to love. I had found the way ahead and was managing to keep one foot in front of the other, but there was something I had forgotten—the second part of Jesus' great commandment, 'Love others as you love yourself'.

I was doing okay with the 'others' part, but I hadn't really thought too much about loving myself. In keeping everyone in the family from falling apart, unfortunately I, myself was falling apart.

In the three or four months following Cameron's diagnosis, I had a weekly babysitting date with my mother in law. I would drive the half hour to her house, drop Cameron and the baby off and then head to the shopping centre.

It was a good time to catch up on any business I needed to do because I had already discovered that it was impossible trying to take Cameron on any kind of shopping trip. But after everything was done, I would head on down to my favourite cafe.

It became a little ritual. Every week I looked around for an armchair table and then ordered a pot of Earl Grey tea and a piece of toasted pistachio and cranberry loaf with butter. I settled in to my chair, pulled out whatever book on autism I had to hand, ate my toast, drank my tea and quietly cried my head off.

I had done some reading about grief and I knew that expressing the feelings and scheduling specific 'grieving' times were supposed to be helpful. This hour in the coffee shop was when I gave myself permission to feel my sadness and get out some of my tears. I don't usually enjoy crying, but I actually looked forward to it all week.

Unfortunately, crying for an hour a week for three months was nothing like enough time to 'get over' my sadness about my son's disability. I felt like I could have cried all day every day for years, and it would still not be okay. I put on my strong face and coped in front of most people, but I knew underneath that I was not alright. Life had to continue, however, so I held myself together and carried on.

Of course, there were good things. When we moved after Bible college, I was thankful to be in a very liveable house right in the centre of town. The people in the congregation were very friendly and we were warmly welcomed. Our daughter found friends almost immediately and everyone loved the baby. My family were helping us pay our bills for autism remediation, which included not only RDI, but also homeopathy and supplements, and were taking Cameron for the occasional weekend. I knew that a quieter life out of the city was definitely going to be better for us all.

Little things gave us hope, like the day that Cameron first played an imaginative game and pretended to be a cat all day. I patted him on the head and called, 'here kitty cat' to his obvious delight.

There were also improvements in his dressing habits and toilet training. In April of that year, I wrote in my blog, "Some day… in a few months… I might not have to buy nappies anymore!"

His language was also improving. For a long time, I despaired of ever hearing anything from him except 'Thomas the Tank Engine' over and over again, but one day he began giving me a running commentary on everything he was doing. "I'm going up the stairs." "He's eating his dinner." I could tell when he was using his own original language as compared to a script because it was a little more stilted and his intonation a little more awkward. But it was appropriate and original, and that was all I cared about.

Every time we saw my parents they assured me that he was making progress. They could see him beginning to acknowledge and enjoy them. They could see him communicating more, being more social and understanding more of what was going on around him.

I could see the progress too, and I was happy about it. But there was still a problem.

I still wasn't dealing very well with the whole concept of my child having autism. Yes, I knew that God was teaching me things. But honestly, sometimes when I told myself that it sounded like, "blah blah blah." I was over it. I wanted the lessons to stop. I wanted my son to get better—now.

Even his progress was never enough for me. If I saw him take a step forward, I also thought about all the steps forward that the other children of his age were taking. I saw him constantly falling behind his age peers, even though he was progressing in his own time.

The fatigue of always 'thinking autism' and trying to manage the anxiety and deal with the tantrums also took its toll. I felt like I was living under a constantly dripping tap, wearing away at me every day.

I wrote this in my blog at the time:

My emotions still fluctuate pretty wildly.

Some days I'm just delighted with his progress and feel up and bright about it all. I can see how far he's come. I can remember how far he had to come. He says things like "I've got the hippy-cups Mum". (Hiccups!) On those days, he's cute and adorable and I love him to death.

Other days, I feel down in the dumps and despondent. Sure, he might have improved. But it's a lot of hard work. And there's just so far to go. When he tells me ten times about each and every 'Give Way' or speed limit sign we pass on the way home, I just wish everything would go away. On those days, he's hard work and irritating, and yet I still love him to death.

Each day was different, but I knew that the day was an especially hard one when all I could do was to droop my head on the kitchen bench as I tried to go about my cooking and cleaning. My face got used to its perpetually sad expression, and the nervous twitch in my lip that had begun months prior continued unabated.

It helped that I was making friends in our new town. Many people were willing to listen and ask questions about Cameron. People at church were keen to connect with him, and a few special ones offered specific help. One beautiful lady even made me a gluten-free dairy-free chocolate cake for him in the hopes that he would eat it. (He didn't, but I did.)

A few months after we had moved, I took the plunge and visited the church playgroup. On the outside, everything went well. It was, in fact, a really good playgroup. It was well-run with friendly people, a great leader, nice toys and happy children. Both my boys played well. I had a refreshing cup of tea, and even managed to say no to the delicious chocolate muffins being passed around.

It seemed fine, but I realised when I came home that I was actually angry, annoyed and restless, and determined never to go back. I wondered if there was something wrong with me. Was I ungrateful for the good things I had? Couldn't I enjoy something as normal as playgroup? Why did I feel so bad and horrible?

After a few explosions and tear jags, I realised that it was because I was still jealous of everyone else's 'normal' kids. Plus, I felt like an imposter in a room full of seemingly confident mothers because I felt like I was only just making it through every day. I was inwardly annoyed at conversations that centred around the difficulties of toilet training or nap time because I felt like I had bigger problems.

"Get over yourself," I just wanted to say. "Your kid is going to toilet train eventually, no matter what you do. Deal with it and be grateful they don't have autism or something else wrong."

Although I can write about how I feel, I find it difficult to admit in words that I'm struggling and after a few hours of being the target of my displaced anger that day, my husband had to work hard to dig all of this out of me.

Helpfully, he had just spent a few days at a workshop on depression, so he listened and then diagnosed.

"It sounds like you have 'reactive depression,'" he said.

"But if I had depression, wouldn't it be the same every day? Why am I so extra upset about it today? I mean, why would going to playgroup make me feel this bad?" I argued back.

He reached for his notes from his seminar. "With every big loss, there are lots of small losses," he explained.

"What does that mean?" I asked. It sounded impressive, but I wasn't sure what he was talking about.

"The big loss is the diagnosis of autism," he said. "We get that." I nodded.

"Today's related small loss was not feeling normal at a playgroup," he went on. "We'll probably experience a lot more 'small losses' before we start to feel better."

My husband was right. The accumulated stress and pressure of living daily with Cameron's difficult behaviours, added to a multitude of 'small losses', seemed to build up over time. As much as I tried to be grateful for the many blessings and the help we were getting, it did all seem too hard, too often.

Within a few months of moving, I felt more angry and resentful, less joyful and more morose. I have never been someone who swore, or who approved of swearing, but I had started to swear in my head in ways I had never done before.

I'd hold it together with the kids, make dinner and put everyone to bed, but if I stubbed my toe on the way through the door, a long stream of obscenity would start rolling through my brain. If I knew I was alone I'd growl out the words through clenched teeth.

Somehow using that strong, ugly language helped me express myself and gave me a way to release the pressure. I was feeling big, dark, overpowering emotions and I needed words that would describe them. Even my prayer journals were full of bad language.

After a whole week where I yelled at the children all day and cried on my husband's shoulder all night, he started to say that I needed to go and get some help.

"You're not ok," he told me. "You're angry, you're crying all the time, and you're just not yourself."

"I can't help it," I raged back. "I just feel so sad about it all. I just want my son to be better. I don't see how I can feel better if he doesn't improve."

"Maybe you need to take something just to help you cope a bit better," he suggested. "You know, like drugs or something. You can't go on like this. The kids aren't happy and I can't cope with it either."

I was horrified. In my book, taking anti-depressants was a serious form of weakness. Other people did that, but not me. Before this, I had always pulled myself through somehow, no matter what the problem. But I had to realise that I had been so focused on helping Cameron that I now needed some help for my own life. Reluctantly, I made the appointment.

I sat in the doctor's waiting room for an hour. It was impossible to ever just walk in to an appointment in this surgery, and I had plenty of time to think.

'He'll probably just say I'm making a mountain out of a molehill and he'll say things aren't that bad,' I said to myself. 'I'm not really depressed, I'm just a bit down right now.'

I sat up a little straighter and tried to arrange myself so that when I went in, I could appear together, light-hearted and slightly apologetic about wasting the doctor's time.

The mild-mannered act lasted for approximately thirty seconds once I finally got into the consulting room.

At the doctor's opening question, "So, what can I do for you?" I began to tear up, and by the time the consultation was over I had used a disproportionately large number of his tissues.

I felt like a fool, blubbering all over his desk, but he seemed to take it in his stride.

"I have almost no hesitation in saying that you're depressed," he said sympathetically. "Once you've answered these mood questionnaires we can talk about antidepressant drugs and finding you a good counsellor."

I nodded, of course. What else could I do? The tears were still dripping down into the growing mass of damp tissues in my lap.

"The drugs will stop you feeling like you're desperate all the time and give you enough support so that you can do some good work talking about the issues," he explained. "We'll start you on a low dose to begin with. Don't worry, you're going to be fine."

I walked out in a mild haze. Taking anti-depressants didn't quite seem real. In fact, I almost felt stupid telling my husband that they were what I had been prescribed. But I filled the prescription and swallowed them and proved the doctor was right. They did lift me, almost in the first week. Things started to get brighter. I felt less ugly and growly and life didn't seem quite the trauma that I had felt it to be before.

Now it was time to get some counselling and start talking about what had happened to my son and to me.

* * *

In my humble opinion... the 'admiration reaction'

People sometimes say to me, "Ooh you're brave, I admire you. I just couldn't do that."

While it sounds nice, it doesn't help.

By putting me up on the pedestal of bravery, they keep a myth going that bad things only happen to brave people. They are normal, so hopefully they're pretty safe.

The reality is that you become brave by facing hardship. Hardly anyone starts out brave!

As for the phrase, "I just couldn't do that," well, no-one ever thinks they can do horribly hard things. But if you have to do it, you do it. And if it's something you have to do for your child, you'll do it even more, because you know that no-one else is going to do it.

Admiration looks like support, but it's not the same at all. Someone who admires me doesn't usually want to hear about my tears or anger or despair. They want to keep the myth going that I cope beautifully because I'm a super-mum. They would rather look up to me than put their arm around me and help me pull through.

When I'm told that I'm brave and wonderful, I feel warm and flattered for about a minute, but the admiration actually separates me from the support of my friends and makes things harder in the long run.

If I ever feel tempted to give the admiration reaction to someone, I'll try to keep it to myself and say instead, "Wow—you must feel like you're being very stretched," or, "How can I help you with something?" or, "Tell me how you feel about that!"

15

Angry and bitter on the couch

It was another Sunday morning, and once again I was attempting to keep Cameron from running out of the church building into the car park. We started off in the Sunday school room.

'Perhaps if I stay with him, he might settle down and be part of it,' I mused. 'You never know. It might just work this time.'

It didn't, of course, but I stuck it out as long as I could before his protest noises became disruptive and I felt the need to leave. We parked in our usual spot in the foyer where he had some room to roam, and I chatted to some of the other mothers who were out looking after their littlies.

One of them had just come from the Sunday school room.

"Your little boy is so cute," she said, trying to be friendly.

"Thanks," I replied. "Although, it can be pretty hard work with him. You see, he's got autism spectrum disorder. That's why he wouldn't stay in Sunday school."

"Oh, autism!" she exclaimed. "That's such a gift for you! Those children are really talented in some ways!"

I nodded weakly and attempted a smile, but I felt mad. She had seen me struggle through a 45 minute Sunday school class with him, just trying to get him to stay in the room. Did she really think that was a gift?

The following week, I told my new counsellor about what happened. I had been talking about two main issues with her. The first issue was my intense anger at finding myself facing the burden and the challenge of living with a child with ASD.

"I'm sure she meant to be nice and see the positive side," I explained to my counsellor. "But I'm mad about it. I don't want to sugar-soap autism and make it all nicey-nicey. People only see the 'genius' autistics who can calculate anything, draw exact replicas of cityscapes and learn 30 different languages in a day. But these people are *not* like most people on the spectrum. Not only that, but they are also pretty much dysfunctional in real life!"

I got angrier just thinking about it. "If your only idea of autism is that ASD people have super talents, then you're ignoring the hard stuff that far outweighs the genius," I said. "And then you manage to paint it with a nice brush and not think, 'oh, this is actually a serious problem we need to do something about'."

At that point, I started to cry. "And then, somehow I'm supposed to say in reply to her, 'Oh yes, isn't it wonderful that he has ASD' when actually it's the trial of my life and I find it really, really, really hard and yucky."

"You sound angry," the counsellor said.

"Yes. I'm angry. And I'm tired," I cried at her. "I'm tired of the meltdowns. I'm tired of changing my life around to deal with this. I'm tired of the fact that I give so much time and effort to improving things for him. I'm terrified of the fact that it's going to be life-long. I just don't know how much of this I can take."

"You know that he's improving with what you're doing for him, don't you?" she asked.

"Of course I know that. It's obvious he's improving," I said, sniffling a little. "And I know I should be happy about that. But when I look at other four year olds, they're also improving. Their rate of progress and growing up is still faster than his rate of improvement. So he's always going to be behind! I can never do enough to help him catch up."

I *was* angry. Ever since the diagnosis, I had been furious that autism had become my job, my passion, my future and my lot in life. It didn't seem to fit with my plans or my talents or my interests. It seemed that I didn't have a choice about what happened to me for the rest of my life and I was mad about that too. Talking through the anger was a big part of my counselling sessions.

The second issue was my fear and worry about Cameron's future, together with my sadness that he had this problem.

One week, she challenged me on this.

"What exactly *is* his problem?" she asked. "I don't mean what's his diagnosis, but what is the problem with having autism? How do you see it?"

It was an easy answer. The problem I saw with Cameron having ASD was that I feared that he would never be truly accepted amongst his peers or have equal relationships with them.

"Someone will always have to regulate for him—do the work of the conversation I mean," I explained, "and he will be seen as a burden, a weight. He'll be someone whom other people will tolerate at best, or persecute at worst."

My counsellor seemed amazed at my answer.

"But surely you must know someone with a disability who is happy? Surely?" she asked.

"Well, yes, but that's not really my point," I said. "The point is, do I know anyone with a disability—and I mean a neurological disability—who is truly part of 'the group'? Absolutely not."

Perhaps my ideas were wrong. I didn't know. What I did know was that I had a son who *wasn't* happy. How could he be happy when he was still having six or seven massive meltdowns every day? How could he be happy when he made a move towards playing with another child, and that child walked away from him because he didn't understand what he was talking about? How could he be happy living with chronic anxiety?

I had had people say to me before, "Oh, yes, it must be hard to have an autistic child, but they're content in their own little worlds, aren't they?"

It had made me mad, and sad. If they could have only lived with my beautiful son and witnessed his pains day after day, they would never have said such a thing. I didn't know about other people, but I knew my own child, and I knew he could never be happy without a lot of changes in his life.

What I also knew, and this came from five years of living in a boarding school, was that the children who look the same as the others, but who act or process information differently, or who don't really understand the norms and informal rules—they are the children who suffer.

Children and teenagers can be cruel. They can be merciless to outsiders and vicious to people who don't fit in. I experienced bullying myself for a whole year once when I started a new school and I know the terrible effects it can have on someone's life.

Luckily for me, I was able to adjust to fit in with the group a little better, and over time, the tormenting stopped. Unfortunately, there were still other children at our school who were unable to adjust, and who were at worst, bullied, laughed at and excluded, or at best, patronised or ignored for the rest of their school career.

Certainly, some children are kind and helpful. There are some who will play with the 'different' kids. They'll try to include them a little and even possibly stand up for them here and there. But the simple reality is that to be able to do that, those kind children need to be in an environment where that behaviour is encouraged, and where bullying is not tolerated. And those environments are few and far between.

Even in those cases, though, the outsiders and the disabled children, and the ones who are struggling, have to rely on the kindness of other children. It's not a peer relationship of equals because the kind child is working much harder than the others to keep the relationship going.

I had thought hard about it, and I just wasn't sure if a friendship is really a friendship where one party is 'trying to be nice' or feeling sorry for the other. Surely happiness in friendship only really comes when two people challenge, enjoy and love each other as equals?

A conversation with a friend who has a grown up son with Asperger's syndrome made me think more about it. My friend was fairly frank about his son's lack of social skills.

"Look, he can't relate to his peers well at all," he told me. "But on the other hand, he has a wonderful capacity to really love people. And really—which is more important, right?"

I had taken the question home with me and turned it over for a while. Which indeed, was more important? And what *is* love? If someone can't relate to their peers, how do they show love? How do others show love to you if they can't relate to you? If I could choose either love or relating skills, which would it be? Surely they were so connected that they couldn't be distinguished?

I was unsure and confused and I remembered again what I had started to think about when Cameron was first diagnosed with ASD. Early on, I had started to ask these questions and begun to work out why I was so sad. I wrote in my blog at the time:

Why is it such a big deal to have a child who isn't typical or normal? Why does every prospective parent say 'I don't mind what it is, just as long as it's healthy...'? Why do we all secretly cringe when we see someone who is disabled or challenged or disturbed?

I have spent the last two or three months feeling sad, heavy and dismayed by the idea that my child is going to struggle in life with his understanding and communication. But in stopping to analyse the fears I have for him, I can see that I'm most afraid of other people's reactions to him. I'm worried that he'll be bullied, excluded, laughed at, tormented or just plain ignored.

How do I know he will suffer these things? Because I know my own heart, and I know my own sinful reactions to others who are different from me. I have bullied, excluded, laughed at, tormented and just plain ignored people who were 'imperfect'.

And in doing so, I have shown my own imperfections, which are far more serious, far more deadly and far more vile than any physical or mental disability could ever be. The real human imperfection is the sinful, unloving heart that each one of us carries inside.

If we humans were truly able to love, having a disabled child would not be a cause of sorrow. It might create a few extra challenges, but parents would not fear for their children, and societies would care for them.

Perhaps the 'imperfect people' are part of the world in order to show up everybody else's imperfection.

"That's my fear for Cameron," I told my counsellor. "That's the way I see his 'problem'. I know the world is cruel. And I know he'll probably suffer from it, and he won't understand what is happening to him."

"And I have another fear," I said, slowly. I looked down at my hands. This one was very difficult to admit, even in the privacy of a counselling room.

"I'm terrified that I won't be able to love him because he'll drive me crazy with impatience, or he'll make me embarrassed," I said. "I mean, realistically, I haven't been very successful at loving people like that yet. In fact, I'd probably count that as my biggest failure in my life so far. I'm really impatient and I'd prefer it if those difficult people just went away."

"I've always thought that having people like that around makes me look like a failure in life, you know? I'd rather be thought of as snappy, smart, intelligent and charming. Not the one who has slow, weirdish kinds of people connected to her."

I took a breath and began to cry.

"But if I, his mother, doesn't love him, no-one else is going to," I said. "I'm just scared that my boy will be unloved in this world. And I'm ashamed of myself too—for thinking this way. It makes me just as cruel as the people I'm talking about."

We talked some more, and I cried some more. At the end of the hour, my counsellor left me with a challenge.

"If you are able to accept Cameron as he is, without needing him to be a 'normal' child," she said, "he ultimately will 'need' less from you and you will have a better relationship."

I agreed, but I was still confused. What does 'acceptance' really mean anyway? If I accepted Cameron as he was, did that mean I wouldn't do anything about trying to remediate his autism and improve his neurological function? If you accept someone as they are, does that mean you have to lower your standards? Do I accept my other children as they are? Do I really know how to accept *anyone* as they are, including myself?

It took me a long time to work through these issues. My thoughts and ideas were not simple to sort out. A lot of the time I felt like my brain was a cement mixer, turning, turning,

turning, with a whole mash of hard stuff inside. And it was never going to be a quick construction job either. There were just too many things to process and change.

But I began to consider a number of things.

First, I pondered the fact that God loves me. I began to see my sin and brokenness as my 'disability'. I was stunned, again, to think that God loved me so much, even as a weak, pathetic disabled being, that he gave up his own son to rescue me.

Did God accept me as I am? I had never thought that he did. I had always thought—probably unconsciously—that his object was to make me better and more godly, and that he wasn't happy with who I was at any given point. Once I got to heaven and was 'made perfect', then, finally, he'd be happy with me because the job was done.

I came to realise, however, that in loving me first off, God was accepting me. It was the forgiveness and the rescue that mattered, not the extra polishing bits. Yes, God wanted me to be more like Jesus, but if I could see that as an ongoing gift rather than a requirement for perfection, I would understand more about love.

Next I began to really think about what I wanted and expected, consciously and unconsciously from my children. Our RDI consultant had asked us this question when we first started off with her, and my answer had shocked me. It was hard to even say it aloud.

"I expect that the children will tag along behind whatever important things I am doing," I admitted to her. "I expect them to fit in and be good. I want them to be well-behaved and reflect well on me. I want to be seen as a successful parent."

As the words came out of my mouth, they jarred in my brain. I suddenly realised that my parenting had been all about me.

Did the children look good? Did they behave well? Great. They're upholding the family name. Are they talented? Are they smart? Fantastic. That's another notch in mummy's belt.

And then it occurred to me that most of the 'love' I had ever given out was also all about me. It's easy to 'love' people who make me look witty, good, powerful and attractive. It's a lot harder to love when you're giving more than you get back, or it's inconvenient or it takes away from your reputation.

It was hard to admit that even though I was a 'nice' person, I was essentially unloving. And it was hard to change my habits and thought patterns. But it did begin to happen—slowly.

I began to really listen to all the children, to show them more affection, to spend more time with them and show them that I valued their discoveries and activities without trying to make them improve themselves or be perfect.

I looked at the simple things like the amount of time I spent with them, and even the language I used with them. Was I always wanting more from them? Was there judgment implied, even in compliments? Could I ever just be happy with them in the moment, or was there always something else to do?

I had to give up a lot of my need to be in control, and give up a lot of my focus on achievement.

I also had to give up a lot of my self-image. I had always enjoyed being 'successful' out the front. I was good at public speaking, I was able to start a conversation with anyone, and I enjoyed being busy and organising events and programs.

The fact that I literally couldn't do much at church and in the community now because I had my hands full with looking after Cameron meant that I was weaned off the admiration people often gave me for my public charm and successes.

I had a more realistic picture of myself now that I didn't rely on the highs of other people's opinions for my worth. It was a challenge to accept myself as being imperfect, and to say, 'that's OK. God still loves me anyway.' As I became better at accepting myself as I am it became easier to accept Cameron as he is.

Of course, I still fall over and fail. I still get frustrated and wish things were different. But I'm on a better road, and I'm hopeful that as I understand what God's love really is, my own love will grow even more.

* * *

Depression: it's pretty normal

Carers do it tough overall.

An Australian study in 2007 found that carers suffer from "extraordinary" rates of depression. Mothers of autistic children suffer depressive symptoms much more than other mothers, according to a US study in 1989.

However, another US study in 2007, entitled Resilience and Families of Children with Autism was able to give some pointers as to why some families living with a child with a disability seem to manage better than others. The general findings concerning evidence of family resilience included the significance of the capacity to pull family resources together and to maintain a connectedness and unity.

Some other findings from this study included:

Flexibility and the capacity for good communication one with another were seen as key strengths underlying resilience and for being able to meet changing demands on the family as a whole.

It appeared that around two years were required for many families to come to terms with the situation and to learn to adjust to the particular demands of the autism.

Motivation to help the child progress, along with observational improvements in the child's functioning, were found to be important for the adjustment and cohesion of the family as a whole.

Resilient families can make some positive meaning of adversity. For example, they may refer to the knowledge acquired or some personal quality developed such as an increased sensitivity to small benefits and gifts and achievements, or a greater awareness of and compassion towards individual differences.

Families tended also to speak in terms of a shift in philosophy, and being able to focus upon things that really matter, while not taking anything for granted.

Having a spiritual belief system appeared to be a component of resilience; and nearly half of the respondents made some reference to new spiritual beliefs or the confirmation of existing religious convictions.

Further reading:

Taking care of yourself, taking care of your child with autism:

https://wayahead.org.au/taking-care-of-yourself-taking-care-of-your-child-with-autism/

Stress Reduction Strategies:

https://www.autismtas.org.au/unlock/the-needs-of-the-family/parentscarers/

Information on Government help in Australia:

http://www.autismawareness.com.au/financial-support/centrelink/

Information on NDIS funding in Australia:

https://www.autismspectrum.org.au/content/national-disability-insurance-scheme-ndis

Autism and the effect on parents and siblings:

www.mugsy.org/connor103.htm

16

Praying for healing

Being a big believer in specific prayer, one of the first things I did after Cameron's ASD diagnosis was create a prayer list.

Every month or six weeks I would email prayer points to our interested friends and family. They would pray and then I would update them with answers and ask for more prayer.

A few things were answered completely. A few things were not answered at all. Perhaps the best thing about it was that I knew that people were interested in Cameron and that they wanted to support us.

I asked them to pray for little things like his eating, his tantrums and keeping his jacket on in the cold. I asked them to pray for his relationships with his brother and sister. I asked them to pray for me as I gathered all the strength and creativity I could for our daily RDI sessions.

And then I began to ask them to pray for his healing.

A year after the prayer list began, I wrote to our friends and family:

"I'm very much into asking God to answer specific prayers, as you can see by the prayer points I've written here. And something that would be fantastic for all of us would be for Cameron to be healed of autism.

I have no qualms about asking God to do that. I understand perfectly that he may say no, and it may be the thing that Cameron and we struggle with for the rest of his life, but if you never ask the question, you never know the answer.

If you feel comfortable I'd love you to pray with me for a complete healing of Cameron's autistic spectrum disorder."

The longer that things went on, the more I thought about healing. Every time I found a story about Jesus healing in the gospels, I scoured it for as much information as I could get. I read the description of the very early church in Acts 2, where the disciples did many signs and wonders and the new believers met together every day for teaching, fellowship and to praise and worship God.

"Maybe I'm wrong," I thought, "but I wonder how many chronic illnesses there were in that early church if so many signs and wonders were being done then. I wonder how many children were left to scrabble around for the medical help they so desperately needed. I bet it would have been impressive to the people around them to see the power of God at work in chronic cases."

I wasn't a theologian. I didn't know how theologians read the healing stories and the signs and wonders in the New Testament. I couldn't say who was right and who was wrong on the debates about miracles today.

The simple things I did know were that God loved me, and Jesus was powerful, and the Bible encouraged, no, commanded, me to bring everything before God in prayer.

A verse that had been very meaningful for me for years was Psalm 37:4 which so beautifully says to 'delight yourselves in the Lord, and he will give you the desires of your hearts.'

"God, the desire of my heart is for my boy to be okay," I prayed, crying one night. "I couldn't get a bigger desire than that. Please, you know that I have delighted in you all my life. You are my life. Could you do this for me? I know that you want me to learn to love people through all of this. I know that's the lesson here. But I've learned so much already that I feel turned inside out. And if you do heal him, I won't forget to keep learning it. Honest. Plus, I'm tired. I'm so tired of all of this. I don't know how long I can keep going with no ending in sight. I'm desperate for a solution. And you're the only one who can provide the solution."

The turning point came for me the week that I was on the roster to give a children's talk in church. The Bible reading that had been assigned was the story of the blind beggar in Mark chapter 10.

The beggar hears that Jesus is passing by and he begins yelling to him, ignoring all good manners or social acceptability. People tell him to be quiet, but Jesus hears it and asks for him to come to him. When blind Bartimaeus stands in front of him, Jesus asks, "What do you want me to do for you?"

Bartimaeus' answer is simple. He wants to see.

Yes, a blind beggar wants his sight. He doesn't justify it. He doesn't explain it. He doesn't ask for an alternative means of income just in case Jesus decides not to heal him. He knows that Jesus is his only hope for a cure, and he does everything he can to get himself in the place of healing.

Jesus' answer is also short and simple. He doesn't give sermons. He doesn't require anything else of the man standing in front of him. He just says, "Your faith has healed you. Go in peace."

I read the story and wept. I knew that if Jesus had been walking the earth now, I would be the person yelling and screaming to get to him, with my poor, beautiful boy in tow. I would pay whatever it cost and I would travel however long it took to get help from Jesus for my child because I knew that he could and would do it.

'If I can stand up in church and teach children this story, and say, "Hey kids, Jesus is powerful," then surely I'm a hypocrite if I don't act on what I know,' I thought to myself. 'This is it. I'm going to take my son to Jesus and ask him to heal him.'

My birthday was coming up in a few weeks, and I decided to do something a little bit unusual. I wanted to pray with other people, and I wanted to make a statement that showed my prayer was a public act of faith in God. So with Andrew's advice and blessing, I sent out these invitations:

You're invited to help celebrate Cecily's birthday in a very special way!

No presents please! Here's why...

The best birthday present anyone could give Cecily would be healing for Cameron from his anxiety and autism, so we're inviting you to join with us for a prayer time. We'll be specifically asking God for healing and neurological health for him. Join us on Friday at our place for a light dinner of soup and buns and birthday cake followed by prayer.

It felt like a bold move. And in the days leading up to the prayer party, I felt scared and nervous. There were more than a few 'what if's?' floating around in my mind.

What if God didn't heal him? Would I be angry or would I really be alright with it? What would it do for his big sister's child-faith to have a 'no' answer? Could we afford to pay the financial and emotional costs of living long-term with autism? Would God still give me the strength I needed to keep going on this never-ending marathon?

What if God did heal him? Would I tell it far and wide and then feel like I was boasting? How could I justify having God heal my child and not the other ten children I know with ASD? Would I suddenly have a ministry of healing? Would I forget what I had learned and just go back to my old ways?

I prepared by re-reading all the gospel healing stories, studying the requests and the reactions of those healed, as well as what Jesus said to them. I prayed continuously, letting God know what I was planning, and what I would like him to do (as if he didn't know anyway!) I tried to examine my motives and to be honest and confess ungodly thoughts to God.

The evening finally came. I cooked soup until it was coming out my ears and ordered bread rolls to feed an army. At six o clock 30 adults from our church, with many more children, crammed into our house for food and fellowship, before meeting in a circle and petitioning God together.

We decided it would be good if I started off the prayer time, so I pulled out my pre-prepared piece of paper and read my request out loud. It was hard to pray when all I wanted to do was cry, but I knew that we were all crying to God together.

These were the things I said to God, whose love had sustained me for years, and whom I had tried to serve to the best of my pathetic ability since I was a child.

Dear God,

I'm here tonight, with all these people, with some very specific requests to make of you.

If Jesus was walking around somewhere in bodily form, I'd be one of the visiting mothers bringing her sick child to you. I would go around the world just to find you and ask you to heal my son because I know that you can.

These are the things I know about you: You are kind. You are compassionate. You take time for people. You are powerful. You can heal. You have healed. You heal people today. If you were standing here in the body, I'd be on my knees before you, holding out my child and saying, "Please, please heal his brain. Please heal his body." In fact, I wouldn't be asking, I'd be begging.

Lord, these are the things the autism does to him. He can't cope with changes. He throws tantrums over small things. He bosses. He speaks in scripts. He obsesses over toys and tv shows. It is really hard for his brother and sister to relate to him. Unless he is healed he won't be able to live independently. He won't have any friends. He won't be able to relate to people. Lord, his body can't process food properly. He won't eat properly. He lacks good nutrition.

Please—please heal his brain. Remove the autism. Create the connections in the brain that he needs. Take away his anxiety.

Lord, I know what you are teaching me through the autism. I know that you have been teaching me to love other people. I know that you have given me patience out of all of this. I know that you have given me an empathy with suffering people that I did not have before. I want to say thank you—a genuine thank you for these things. You have brought good out of evil. I know I still have a lot to learn, but I think I can now learn them without autism.

Now I'm asking you to heal him.

For his own sake. For the children's sake too. You know how they are both suffering because of the autism and the anxiety. Please heal this child and give the other two a faith which can move mountains because of what you've done.

And please heal him for my sake. I'm tired. It's only been three years really, but it's been every day for three years where I just haven't known what to do, or how to do it, or how to get on with him. It's been a grind many, many days. I do feel desperate so often.

And please heal him for the sake of all the people around him—the local community and his friends and teachers and contacts. I would love to say, "We prayed and God healed him in answer to our prayers.

God is good!" What a testimony that would be. For your sake please heal this child.

I know you're hearing me. I'm really asking you to do a big thing here—although it's small for you. Please would you do it. And, I'm going to really stick my neck out here and ask you to do it fast. Make the change as big as possible in as short a time as possible. That's what you did so often for the people who came to Jesus.

Finally—Lord, I believe, help my unbelief.

I organised this meeting because of Jesus' words: 'this kind can only come out by prayer.'

Amen.

When everyone had said their piece, the prayer meeting broke up. We all hugged and tried to bring a bit of humorous normality back to the deeply emotional atmosphere.

As people left, they said things like, "We've never done anything like this before," or, "That was really special. Thank you for your honesty." Our 70 year-old neighbour pressed into my hand a wood spoon with a cross carved into it that he had made for me. "We love you, and we love Cameron," he said, with tears in his eyes.

The meeting was over. And now we would see what the effects would be. Would Cameron be healed? Would it be immediate, or slow-going? Would I be able to praise God for whatever answer he gave to my question? Or would I find it more difficult to cope with a 'no' than I had thought?

17

Dealing with the aftermath

It turned out that after the prayer meeting, I wasn't happy with a 'no' answer.

It turned out that I felt achingly, bitterly, obscenely and roaringly angry with God. For months and months and months.

In the days after the prayer meeting, I watched Cameron closely. Nothing seemed to have changed for him and certainly, nothing had changed for me in the way I related to him. I watched him closely for the next few weeks. There were the usual few steps forwards and steps backwards. We made some progress and had some regressions. It was pretty much the regular routine.

"Fine," I thought to myself, "God didn't heal him immediately. So it's a 'no' answer. I'm alright with that. After all, I always said that you would never know the answer unless you asked the question. Yes, I'm disappointed, but I guess God has something else in mind."

But I still couldn't get it out of my head. "Perhaps if I give up, I'll be the doing wrong thing," I thought. "After all, Paul prayed three times to get rid of his thorn in the flesh."

I heard about a healing meeting taking place at an Assemblies of God church an hour's drive away. One of our biggest prayer supporters, a godly ex-missionary woman, offered to come with me, so the two of us took Cameron with us to a long and noisy service that I would never have gone to in previous years. It wasn't my style, and I had reservations about the preaching, but there was not much else around that seemed useful so I took the plunge.

Again, Cameron's progress followed its usual up and down course but there was no real change to be seen at all.

I tried one final avenue. A minister friend in a different denomination knew a group involved in a fairly intense prayer ministry. I packed Cameron into the car and drove to Sydney so that he and I could be prayed for once again.

I saw some gains, but nothing spectacular, and certainly nothing like what I had hoped for.

"That's three. That's it. I'm done with this," I said to myself. But I really wasn't happy.

The feelings built up over a few months. The first thing that made me realise that something was wrong was the fact that I now read my Bible with a cynical attitude.

'God's powerful? Great. Then why didn't he show his power when I asked him to?' I thought to myself.

'God loves me? Well, how come I feel like I've been completely ignored? I wouldn't do that to my own children.'

'God has my best interests at heart? So how come I'm depressed and floundering and unable to cope?'

As time went on, I gave up reading it because I felt too angry. I could go to Bible study and church, and even encourage other people who were struggling, but inside I wasn't okay. It was easy enough to appear as though I was coping, but it was hard to admit the truth of what I was really thinking to my friends, especially because my husband was in the ministry. I wasn't supposed to have lapses of faith, or whatever this was that was happening to me.

I kept it to myself for several reasons. First, I felt like I had taken enough sympathy and support and love from everyone already. It was one thing to have people cry with me for a short time-frame. It was another thing to ask for support for a chronic, unsolvable, ongoing problem. The second reason was that I didn't think that anyone would have anything that they could tell me that would help.

I knew, at least in my head, that God is good, that all things work together for good for those who love him, that God is allowed to say 'no' to prayer requests, that I perhaps might not be able to see the bigger picture, that God is sovereign and we have to trust him, that Paul didn't have his thorn in the flesh removed, that I need to be content, trust, pray, read the Bible and so on and so forth.

I knew these things. The problem was that I still felt mad and angry. And the feelings just weren't going away no matter what I said, thought or did.

I wrote in my blog:

Do I really think God loves me? I'm not sure right now, to be honest. Why wouldn't he answer my specific prayer with a yes? I feel like I'm the one who has been doing all the work to help my son get better—not him.

And then I feel guilty for saying things like this.

I hope that in the next 12 months I will start to really believe in God's love for me... I want to be the person who shines naturally with the love of God, not who hides her swear words under her breath and puts on a 'cheerful' face for others (which later gives her a headache).

I went through a cycle of avoiding God, repenting and praying for forgiveness, and trying to get over the anger, only to find that it wouldn't go away, whereupon I would avoid God again, and continue the cycle.

Things would feel fine for a while, but then something would trigger the anger and I'd spend days feeling low and emotionally fragile as I cried out again and again in rage and pain.

There was no immediate cure and no magic bullet to get rid of my feelings, or regain the joy and trust I had had in previous years. The healing happened, inch by inch, over many, many months, and was usually brought about by yet another emotional crisis.

More than a year after the prayer meeting, we visited friends from Bible college days. My husband and his friend were talking about what was happening in their respective churches and the subject of healing services came up.

My friend said, "There's a healing guy coming to our suburb. I want to go and see what's going on. I know where he'll be coming from because I've read his stuff, and I know it won't be much good."

Immediately I felt prickly. Emotions started boiling up inside me. I felt like running away or lashing out. And I was surprised. I didn't realise I still had such strong reactions.

The conversation went on about how a lot of healing 'road shows' are not based on biblical theology and get into a whole lot of stuff that isn't helpful or biblical. I agreed, but I still needed to say, in a very petulant and defiant tone,

"Well, I wish we could hear some good teaching about healing sometimes. I wish healing was a part of *our* theological tradition."

"But in what form?" asked our friend, genuinely curious. "How would you like to see it done?"

"I don't know," I shrugged, sulking. "I just wish it was."

Our friend seemed a little confused. He didn't quite know what my attitude was all about, and I didn't have energy to proceed, so I left the room. Later, I still felt churned up, so I tried to explain why I was speaking so strongly.

"Last year I spent months praying about Cameron's healing from autism," I told him. "I invited a whole lot of families from our church to pray specifically for his recovery. I asked God for a miracle, and nothing came of it."

Then, of course, I started to cry.

"Obviously, I just feel really angry about it. I'm angry with God still. Not at my core, but around the edges I am," I said, a touch incoherently.

He listened to me, and then asked a really good question. "How do you want people to respond to what you've just told us?"

"I don't know," I shrugged and mumbled, still winking back tears. "I just don't know."

It took a while before I could sort out what I was feeling and thinking. A few hours later, driving home in the car, I figured it out a little better and told my husband a garbled version of this:

Christians in our circles spend a reasonable amount of time rejecting unbiblical healing ministries, and usually for good reasons. We argue that they get people focusing on things that are not gospel-centred, they present a distorted view of God's reality and they emphasise celebrity 'healers' and exciting 'miracles' over the every-day journey of following Christ through up and down.

But I wonder if our language and our thinking and indeed our practice might change if we came at it from another angle—the angle of suffering with the people who attend these services.

Many, many people go to those things because they are desperate. They are suffering greatly, they feel as though they are at the end of their rope and they don't know how they can go on bearing their heavy load. People with chronic conditions seek out healers because they've tried everything else. They live with a burden of desperation and pain that they can't carry on their own. They don't like it, they want to be free of it, and they see Jesus in the gospels, who healed so many and so completely and they truly believe that God can heal them.

I know, because that's how I felt.

Maybe if we could see and feel the desperation that 'healing-seekers' live with, perhaps that might more fully inform our preaching, our church practice, our pastoral care, our words of encouragement, our visiting, our acts of mercy.

Perhaps if we listened more and gave healing-seekers permission to feel desperate, to be angry and to doubt *and* supported them while they expressed their emotions, perhaps that would be half of the healing.

There's a line that many healing ministries push to justify any miracles that don't happen. It's the old one of, "You don't have enough faith, that's why God didn't heal you."

But there is also a line, however indirect and unspoken, that other Christians hold. It can stop us from having to deal with the misery and the anguish of the healing-seeker.

It goes like this: 'If the desperate, pathetic, searching individuals really truly understood God's sovereignty and his grace as expressed in the gospel, and as preached faithfully from the pulpit, then they wouldn't feel as bad as they do, and they wouldn't be weak and wavering and tempted into attending dodgy healing meetings.'

What's the problem? On one side, they say that people don't have enough faith. On the other side, they say that people don't have enough theology.

And both times, the person with the burden too great to carry alone is left feeling like a failure as well as still having to deal with whatever chronic condition it is that they desperately want to have healed.

With great nervousness and trepidation, I wrote all of this down and posted it on my blog, including:

What do I want from the church?

I'd love to see healing and health and sin and sorrow preached about from the pulpit, from someone who really understood suffering and travail. I am glad that chronically and temporarily ill are prayed for every week. I'd like to see it more emphasised. I would like to see people taking time to carry each other's burdens. I'd like to see specific healing prayer meetings held for those who request it or perhaps held regularly. I'd like to hear the word 'healing' spoken in positive, innocent tones in conservative churches and not accompanied by an eye-roll.

How do I want people to react if I tell them I'm suffering and I'm angry with God?

Well, I don't want 'right' answers. They don't help much when I feel terrible. I'd really like a hug, if it's appropriate. I'd like permission to express myself. I'd like no judgment, please. I'd like sensitive questions to help me find ways to tell why and what I'm feeling. I'd like an offer of help with my chronic problem. I'd like them to pray for me. And when I've had enough of talking about, it, I'd like them to be able to move on and not hark back to the subject every time they see me!

It was hard to put myself out there and express how I'd been feeling for so long. I posted it that night, feeling raw, naked and bruised. It was no surprise that I slept badly, had angry dreams and woke up cranky as a bear the next morning.

In fact, I didn't really feel any better and as I headed out the door for my early morning walk, I was still worked up.

It's good to walk and think. Some of the emotional energy gets pounded into the ground as I go. As I breathed more deeply and worked harder in my body, I began to think about the 30 years that I had been a Christian, trusting Jesus.

"Has it come to this, that I reach this mountain in my life and my faith just stops?" I asked myself. "Is my Christian life just going to stall here? Will I be stuck in bitterness and anger for the rest of my days? Am I going to let my faith fade away? In another 30 years will I look back and say, 'Well, I had faith until it got too hard, so I just let it go?'"

For years I had taken pride in my faith in God. I had been strong, I had been committed, I had been devout. I had gone against the crowd, I had been wise (apparently) in the choices I've made, I had been sensible and mature. I enjoyed my faith. It defined me.

As I stomped along, trying to think this all through, it struck me that the faith I thought I had has been stripped bare. It's been taken off me. I said to myself, 'Maybe, in the end *my* faith is pretty much worthless."

And then the verse about the refiner's fire popped into my head.

See, I have refined you, though not as silver; I have tested you in the furnace of affliction. Isaiah 48:10

It struck true. I'm being refined in the fire of affliction, and there's not much of *my* faith left.

As I turned into our driveway, I thought, "It will be okay. At the core, I'm not angry, and God has given me faith, and I have nowhere else to go, and all I have to do is just keep putting one foot in front of the other on God's pathway."

'Perhaps just 'being there' is faith as much as good feelings or strength of conviction or enjoyment of the spiritual life,' I thought. 'God is burning what I've built up and is replacing it with something that is stronger and purer and more real. The failure of my faith to trust God is not really a failure because *my* faith can never do it perfectly. Only the faith God gives me will be able to do it.'

It was another small step on the long path back.

More small steps came through more tears and crying.

One night I cried in bed after a difficult day, pleading with God for Cameron's future. "Why have you given him this burden? How can we carry it with him?" I asked, and the verse from 1 Corinthians 12:24 came to me about treating him with special honour. I held onto it carefully for the next few weeks.

Another night I shared how I felt with my women's Bible study. "But maybe you can't see the big picture, and maybe God is doing something else with you," said one dear friend.

"Look, I know," I said. "I know the reason God gave me this. It's to teach me about loving people," and I told them all about when God spoke to me even before Cameron's diagnosis.

'Perhaps God's answering *that* prayer still, rather than the healing prayer,' I thought. 'Perhaps he wants to make me even more able to love than I ever thought possible. Perhaps you can only really love truly in hard, unending situations where there is no solution.'

Again, it helped for a little while.

Finally, I poured out my heart on email to a friend who had been through a similar dark night of the soul.

Her reply was like gold, and by this stage I was ready to hear it.

Like you, 'I knew all the answers' and 'there wasn't a better option to live for'. Except that doesn't make sense. Either I didn't know all the answers, or there was something better to live for. Here's some tough love: you (and I) don't know all the answers. Let God's word wash fresh over you, even if it's just a sentence that you ruminate over in a busy day. Ask God for a pearl that you can take with you into each day and let it become precious to you again.

Like some ancient saint said, "Lean your elbows on the window sill of heaven each morning and gaze into the face of your God, then with the vision in thy heart turn strong to meet the day."

Having said that, though the Bible speaks truth, grief often renders it unreal. You've spent months alone in pain, your heart is angry, you feel God is unjust and absent and you're soldiering on ministering to other souls in his name.

In grief we need people to hold our hands, sometimes not to even say or quote anything. People who just drop off food and flowers, the basics of beauty and life. People who write simply, 'your broken-hearted sister'.

I don't want to be the quoting sage. I am your broken-hearted sister.

And yet it's times like this that shake us into knowing the real God. The one who doesn't direct his plan according to our desires, where we are at the centre of things.

More tough love: I am praying you are overcome with how impotent you are before the Almighty God whose plans are 'to display HIS glory' (Isaiah 61:3) and on a scale you can't imagine.

I am praying that in your questioning, grief and anger you would be drawn to the cross where the deepest pain, "My God, my God, why have you forsaken me?" is your cause for the greatest joy.

I am learning. I will probably and hopefully always be learning. I hoped that God would answer my prayers for miraculous healing, but I know that he has me, and my beautiful son, in his arms regardless. With all my questions and disappointments and imperfections, today, I'm happy to stay there.

* * *

In my humble opinion... meeting the needs

What an autistic child needs

- *Time, space and understanding*

- *Calm conversation which invites, but doesn't require a response. Make statements rather than asking questions and don't overtalk.*
- *People who really love him or her*
- *An occasional invitation to a birthday party*

What a parent of an autistic child needs

- *Friends who will listen to their struggles without having to say something that makes it all okay*
- *Friends who will stick it out with them for the long term. Autism is a chronic condition.*
- *People who show love and friendship towards the autistic child.*
- *The occasional night or afternoon off.*
- *Support with practical things like housework, babysitting or even money if things are really tough or tight.*
- *Understanding, especially at times like Christmas or family events which might be stressful for the child.*
- *A no-judgment attitude towards what may appear to be antisocial behaviour by the child.*
- *A lot of quiet, background prayer.*

What the church can do to help

- *Ask the parents what they need, and find a way to meet those needs.*
- *Roster on or pay for a helper either during Sunday school or after church so that parents can listen to a sermon or chat to people.*
- *Pray regularly for healing for the child and strength for the family.*
- *Be aware of the stages of grief and mindful of depression.*

DEALING WITH THE AFTERMATH

- *Support the siblings.*

18

It'll take a miracle

It took me a while to work out, and then accept, that God *is* answering our prayers. But rather than giving us an immediate, astounding, earth-shattering answer, he's doing it in a way that is more in line with the principles of love.

The Bible says that love is patient, love is kind, love always hopes and love never gives up. Cameron's progress has required patience, kindness, hope and perseverance from both Andrew and I. And while it has been bit by bit, step by step, and sometimes not always easy to see, it has been definitely been progress.

One of the very first things we had to do when we began therapy with Cameron was to write a 'mission preview statement'.

"What on earth is that supposed to mean?" I asked our RDI consultant.

"I want you to think about what you hope for Cameron in say, two years," she explained. "Write a little story that describes what you'd like to see happen in your family life with him."

"How is that going to help?" I asked, doubtfully.

"You'd be surprised. It gives you a goal to work towards. It helps you visualise how things could be," she said. "And when you get there, hopefully, you'll see that what you were aiming for has happened."

I was sceptical, and my first attempt at a mission preview was written in technical language and arranged in bullet points.

"No," said our consultant. "Not like that. Make it a story, a description. Come on, you're supposed to be a writer. Imagine what life is going to be like for you guys."

I gritted my teeth and wrote what I considered to be a fanciful, unrealistic, over the top, ridiculous prediction of life in our family in two years time.

"Seriously. This is going to take a miracle," I muttered as I handed it in. This is what it said:

It's the end of Cameron's first week at school. We're all walking home together.

"What did you do today?" I ask.

"I did a great painting," he says. "And then I played with two boys at recess. It was really fun."

We walk calmly through the front door and head in for afternoon tea.

"Can I have an orange please Mum?" he asks.

"Sorry, I don't have any oranges left. Would you like a banana?" I say.

"Okay," he says.

After they eat, Cameron says to Max, "Let's go ride our bikes. I'll pull you in the wagon. Jasmine, do you want to come too?"

The three of them run off together to play quietly outside with no yelling.

Firstly, I didn't believe he'd ever make it to school, let alone survive there.

Then, I didn't believe he could ever walk home from anywhere without yelling or protesting.

I never thought he could answer my questions, or express an opinion about something and I certainly didn't believe he'd ever do a painting, or play happily as equals with other children.

I never thought he could get through the front door without a meltdown, and I certainly never expected him to eat new food, let alone cope with a change in the menu.

I did not believe that he would play happily with his brother, nor think to invite anyone else to play, or take himself outside to play.

But things changed. We continued with our RDI program as our main therapy and he went to preschool. I did a few extra things with him like see a homeopath regularly and take him to a kinesiology for a 'Brain Gym' program. I saw him make good progress with both.

When he turned four and a half, we began to think about what Cameron would do for school. That year, he would have been eligible to attend an early intervention unit through one of the public schools in the area.

It was a program that was a mix between preschool and school but in miniature, with two staff to eight children. It looked like a good service but I didn't want to risk exhausting him or raising his anxiety too much to work on developmental objectives.

We kept him at home for the year and continued with his RDI work and his regular preschool days. In desperation and fear, I even read up about home schooling. I felt like I had a small reprieve when I realised I didn't officially have to enrol him until he turned six. With an August birthday, that gave me an extra half year before I would have to do anything official.

At the end of that year, 2008, I wrote a summary in my blog.

We've seen good progress this year although it was a bit hard to believe that in the middle months somehow.

His speech is better. He is having more conversational interactions. He understands more. He is asking questions about things. He is saying, "Look at me," and being motivated to join in games with others. The other day we went to the park where he saw a little boy from preschool. "Eden. I got a Woody toy for Christmas. Eden. Do you want to play with me?"

He's better with people that he knows if he's in the mood for them. He quite likes Mr W next door and usually says hello and goodbye and makes a comment or asks a question. Today he asked for his grandparents to come and visit him. He knows the relationships between different people.

He shows great interest in what others are doing. Tonight our daughter was out with friends at the fireworks. "Where is she?" he asked. I gave a vague answer but that wasn't specific enough for him. "Where did they go?" and, "What is she doing?"

He can cope with more noise and chaos than previously, although it's still not a whole lot.

He can deal better with transitions. He doesn't yelp any more. He can get in and out of the car without hassles (most of the time). He doesn't have to do his specific rituals at the front door any more.

And I can deal better with it too. My everyday sadness has lifted somewhat. I feel more optimistic for him. I find myself treating him more like the other children than I used to. I expect more from him, and I don't panic or shut down as much as I used to.

So looking back, all in all it has been a good year, even though at times it seemed impossible to go on. I don't want to sound falsely happy as though it has all been great and steady progress and everything is on the up and up. There was a period where I really wondered if I could go on with this, and one or two episodes where I felt as low as I have ever felt, and in fact, really truly understood how some parents either harm their children or engage in self-harm.

Thankfully, though, with help and grace from God and from people, I have made it through the year and I'm ending it with optimism.

That's a real blessing and probably the greatest miracle yet.

2009 was the year that Cameron was supposed to start school, but I knew and our preschool teacher knew that he could not cope with going. After a lot of talk with the preschool, they agreed to continue with him for the year. To keep the education system happy, I had decided that I would officially 'home school' him when he turned six but basically just continue on with what we had been doing.

I was absolutely delighted when he came home from preschool after the first week and started talking about his friend, Xavier. A friend? Could that be real? The staff confirmed it. Xavier was a year younger, but he and Cameron had clicked from day one, and played together at every opportunity.

I was also delighted when we finally ticked off every objective in the fourth stage of the RDI program. Things were moving along nicely.

So far, so good for my plan.

The complication came when a job change came up for my husband. For a minister, a job move usually means a move of house and location too. And often, for children, a different school and a whole new set of friends.

I had very mixed feelings. On one hand, I knew it would be the right thing for my husband because it would be seriously less stressful for him, but on the other hand, I really didn't want to shift Cameron, especially now he had a friend. I didn't know if another preschool would take him now that he was school age but I didn't think he'd manage at school. I also didn't want to load the extra stress of moving and making new friends onto myself again.

Amazingly, in the weeks of searching and applications and interviews and negotiations, Cameron made incredible progress.

One night he stood behind me while I typed on my blog and dictated this:

"Cameron has new shoes. Cameron is a brand new boy. Max is a brand new boy too. Max has new shoes too. Cameron goes really faster. Max goes faster too. Cameron has a new big striped shirt."

It was true. He was wearing jeans and a new shirt. And I had managed to convince him that he would go faster if he had fast shoes. After two and a half years wearing crocs, day in and day out, he finally had socks and joggers on his feet.

A few days later, I took him with me to our daughter's youth group for a parents' evening. A five-year old boy that he knew slightly was also there. The two of them spent an hour playing together. Sure, it was simple stuff like 'tip' and pulling and pushing a heavy box but they were really relating. My attention, which was supposed to be directed to my daughter and the youth group was happily (if secretly) diverted to watching my boy play. I felt exhilarated.

In the next month, through a series of little miracles and coincidences, Andrew accepted a post at a small village not far from the town we were at. It seemed ideal. It was a job that was perfectly suitable for Andrew's gifts and talents, and close enough to our friends so that I wouldn't be too lonely. The children were happy too. Who wouldn't be when the business next door to the church property was a lolly shop?

And directly across the road from our house was a little country primary school.

"It's a great school," I heard so many people say as we prepared to move. "It's friendly, it's accepting of children with disabilities, and it's small."

And I was feeling so optimistic with Cameron's progress that for the first time ever, I thought he might actually be able to make it to school, but only, strictly on a part-time basis.

I made an appointment to talk to the principal. I took reports, papers and RDI objectives. I even asked our preschool teacher to come with me and add her support. I had my gloves on and my sleeves rolled up and I was ready to fight for what I thought was best for my child.

It was incredible. I talked and the principal listened. He asked some good questions and then said to me, "So, what do you want him to do?"

I was a little taken aback. Surely it couldn't be this easy?

"Um, for him to go to school three days a week please. Only a couple of hours a day."

His answer was simple. "Sure, okay."

And so, a month later, my sweet, precious boy started school.

It was a challenge for all of us. I was moved when Jasmine came to me in tears the week before they began and said, "Mum, what if there's a bully at school and they pick on him?"

"Honey, if anything like that happens, I will be in that school like a flash," I said, giving her a hug. "I will be a mother bear, and I will not let it happen. And if worst comes to worst, I'll bring him home and home school him. You don't need to worry. I'm more concerned about it than you are!"

It was challenging for him to begin with and it took him six months before he really settled down. At one stage he said to his teacher, "You're fired", and told his aide that she should leave because she was no good.

Every morning that I took him required all the creativity and patience that I had. We ended up being regular before-school patrons of the lolly shop. I could bribe him out of the house for a lolly treat and then it was relatively simple to walk across the road together. On the days where it was impossible to get him there, I asked him to at least come and tell his teacher, and then tried to do something with him at home.

But as time went on, he grew in competence and felt more comfortable. We extended his hours until he was staying three full days.

One day towards the end of term four, he suddenly worked out that the other children in his class came to school five days a week.

"I'm going to be a Monday to Friday boy too," he said. And in the last week of Term Four, he managed to make it to school full time for the first time ever.

Of course, I had to make sure that we still had time for RDI, and I had to keep the long term objectives in view. It helped a lot to have a nurturing school culture, an understanding and flexible teacher and an interested, imaginative and competent teacher's aide. I became more and more hopeful that school would be a good thing moving ahead.

The original mission preview statement that I was so sceptical about was supposed to be a prediction for Cameron's progress and our family life in two years time. We didn't quite make it in that time frame, but after three years, these things happened.

It was his second week of Year One, and only the third week that he had ever stayed at school for the full five days. I wrote in my blog:

As I walked through the school playground at pick up time, Cameron spotted me out the classroom window.

"Mum, mum! We're doing art. Look at my pictures!" He raced up, very excited, to show me what he had done. Later, as we walked calmly through the front door, I asked him what else he did at school.

"I played with Nathan and Kiri," he said as we went into the

kitchen. "We were heroes. Ash and Sarah were the villains. Hey, I'm hungry. Can I have an muesli bar?"

"No," I said, "but I have some pretzels and some watermelon."

"Okay," he replied.

After he had eaten, I said to both boys, "You guys can go ride your bikes if you like."

"Okay, mum," said Cameron. "Let's go Max. Where's Jasmine?" And they ran outside to play.

Maybe I have the beginning of my miracle after all.

19

So, what about love?

On that bright and shiny, happy Sydney day, I followed God's prompting and prayed for love. It didn't feel like a life-changing prayer at the time.

Four years later, I felt like I had been battered, bruised and just about turned inside out. I learned more than I ever wanted to learn, did more than I ever thought I could do, and saw myself stretched and broken more than I thought I could have ever survived. I went from being generally happy and joyful to unhappy, depressed and despairing, back to a more subdued but strong, inner peacefulness.

When I looked at the classic passage about love in 1 Corinthians 13, I saw change and progress in myself, but I felt further than ever from perfection!

If I could speak in any language in heaven or on earth but didn't love others, I would only be making meaningless noise like a loud gong or a clanging cymbal. If I had the gift of prophecy, and if I knew all the mysteries of the future and knew everything about everything, but didn't love others, what good would I be? And if I had the gift of faith so that I could speak to a mountain and make it move, without love I would be no good to anybody. If I gave everything I have to the poor and even sacrificed my body, I could boast about it; but if I didn't love others, I would be of no value whatsoever.

Like an immature child, I prayed for these abilities. I wanted to be 'useful' to God, and impressive to others. God showed me so clearly that in the end I knew nothing about him and what he valued.

Love is patient and kind. Love is not jealous or boastful or proud or rude.

Well, I learned a lot more about patience. And kindness. I still strugglde with jealousy and rudeness, but I was put in the situation where it was impossible for me to boast or be proud because I had failed so much.

Love does not demand its own way.

I learned that it's only when you *can't* get your own way that you realize just how much you really, really want it!

Love is not irritable, and it keeps no record of when it has been wronged.

I learned to trade being irritable for telling the truth about my feelings. I learned to hold my tongue and take a deep breath when I felt annoyed. I learned to be calm when everything around me was saying, 'you should lose your cool here!'

It is never glad about injustice but rejoices whenever the truth wins out.

I became a tiger mother, defending her child, and standing up for him whenever he needed it. I felt the injustices towards disabled people far more keenly than I ever did.

Love never gives up, never loses faith, is always hopeful, and endures through every circumstance.

Never is a big word. Always is a bigger word. Endure is just a hard word. There was so much to learn here. My marathon wouldn't be over for a long time and I so clearly didn't have the strength myself to endure, or hope, or hold on. I desperately needed what God would give me.

Love will last forever, but prophecy and speaking in unknown languages and special knowledge will all disappear. Now we know only a little, and even the gift of prophecy reveals little! But when the end comes, these special gifts will all disappear.

When I felt like my talents were underused, that my purpose was tiny and the goals I set would never be reached, it was easier to feel that what I was doing was worthwhile when I read that 'love lasts forever'.

When I was a child, I spoke and thought and reasoned as a child does. But when I grew up, I put away childish things. Now we see things imperfectly as in a poor mirror, but then we will see everything with perfect clarity. All that I know now is partial and incomplete, but then I will know everything completely, just as God knows me now.

If there's one thing I learned, after a lifetime of trying to be good, perfect, multi-talented and very competent, it's that I didn't know everything and I rarely had the answers. Sometimes that was hard to handle. Other times I was grateful.

There are three things that will endure—faith, hope, and love—and the greatest of these is love.

Although I complained and I failed and I dragged my weary feet, I became grateful that God was taking the time and the effort to teach me so much about his greatest enduring gift, love.

20

What's happened since I wrote this book?

Love, Tears & Autism covered the first seven years of Cameron's life, and more specifically, the four years from the time of diagnosis, to his first year of school.

Seven years later, at the time of updating and creating this second edition, Cameron and his brother are in high school, we have a fourth child (a little girl, born when Cameron was seven) and Jasmine is living away from home at university.

Things are different.

Things are *very* different.

For a start, life at home is calmer. The meltdowns are fewer and further apart. When they do come, they are still full on, but nowhere near as noisy as they used to be. We're all better at avoiding trigger points, and Cameron himself is adept at recognising his own reactions and finding ways to help himself calm down.

From being a kid who could hardly talk or express himself, Cameron has become an articulate young man with a huge sense of humour and keen wit. Unfortunately, when he's anxious it comes out as angry words. It's a challenge to remember that for him, rudeness is mostly anxiety. And he's still anxious a fair amount of the time.

He spent a few years making evil-sounding threats which we dealt with by not taking anything personally, and working through them in a calm, logical fashion.

"I'm so angry with you, I'm going to kill you," he told me once, coming into the bathroom while I was in the shower.

"Oh, really." I took a moment to think about it, water pouring over my face. "How do you think you'll do that?"

He paused to consider. "With an axe."

I raised my eyebrows and picked up the soap. His solution was practical. The only problem was we didn't have an axe. I told him this.

"I'll go buy one," he said.

"Yeah, but you don't actually have any money," I pointed out.

He had no comeback. Clearly, I'd crushed his hopes. He left the bathroom, and I didn't hear about my impending death again that day. (Also, I didn't buy an axe for a while.)

Over the years he has also honed his insult-dispensing skills and we have regularly been the recipients of amusing, if terse, notes expressing his displeasure with us.

My favourite was this one: "When I'm king, you'll be sorry."

The notes stopped a little while ago, which I was sad about. They were funny. I kept them, though, and I hope one day he'll enjoy them too.

It's been tricky to have a lot of togetherness as a family over the years. All too often, Cameron couldn't cope with outings. My husband and I became used to splitting up with the kids to take them to different places, depending on needs. This is probably my greatest felt loss over the years. I see other families' holiday photos on social media and feel envious that it's no big deal for them to go out for lunch together, or head down to the beach, or even just go for a walk as a family.

Celebrations like Christmas and birthdays have been tough. For some reason he has found it very hard when he is *expected* to be happy himself, or to be happy for other people. We've taken a three basket approach to these times. He has to attend the celebrations (Basket A), mostly because we literally cannot leave him behind, but if it's too hard to eat at the table or open presents with other people (Baskets B or C), we have become okay with finding other, quieter alternatives for him.

His siblings have had good times and hard times. I love that they really, really want to be his friend and spend time with him, however, they've suffered at the end of his tongue at various points, which has been hard for them to understand. We've always been open about things, and we work very hard on making sure we all tell the truth about our feelings and speak in constructive ways.

School has been an immensely positive experience for Cameron (although he might not express it in those terms. He's variously called school a 'gulag' and a 'prison camp'.) Our primary school could not have been more supportive, more flexible and more wonderful, and I am forever grateful to the staff who listened to us and allowed us to have input into Cameron's time there. The teachers' aide who already worked at the school had been a speech therapist with a great interest in all sorts of therapy for all sorts of issues, and she was very happy to work with him according to RDI principles. I also came over to school every week and took him out of class to focus on some RDI-style activities.

On the last day of Year Six, I wrote this in my blog:

Tonight I am going to Bright Eyes' Year 6 farewell dinner. He will be finishing Primary School and heading to high school in January. Honestly? It's something I never thought would happen. If you'd asked me seven years ago how he was going to get through school, I would have probably cried and said, "He can't do it."

But he has done it. And he's done it well.

I can't tell you the number of things this kid has achieved. Things that I wouldn't have thought possible years ago.

There are the basics: actually getting through the door, in the right uniform, every single day.

And there are the extras: doing the curriculum - and doing it well in general, learning to write, managing kids and noise and chaos, dealing with waiting and frustration and things that are hard.

There are the bonuses - things like coming second in the Regional spelling bee, winning a drawing competition, actually enjoying things, and having a couple of friends.

And there are the impossible dreams - doing cross country, swimming laps, making speeches, acting in plays, doing dance performances, learning the drums.

I am so grateful. Grateful to our marvellous school and its unbelievable staff and support staff who've worked with us and listened to us and modified what needed to be modified, but pushed him when he needed to be pushed. Without this unique and friendly school, his progress would never have been as impressive.

Obviously, I was a nervous wreck when Cameron began Year Seven, going off to High School, especially because (a) he would be wearing a tie and jacket every day, (b) he had to get a bus there and back and (c) he was going without a teachers' aide! We were very careful to choose a school which would get to know him well, and which would deal promptly with any bullying issues, and they have been great. The biggest issue for him in high school has been organisation and we have had to be very involved in helping with homework. But it's been extremely positive overall and he has found some welcoming niches and some friends.

In the seven years since the first version of this book, we have kept on with various therapies and ways to make life better for everyone. We kept up with RDI for about three more years, and then gradually did less and less specific RDI activity, however, the skills and concepts we learned from this incredible therapy are still very much a part of our lives.

We began seeing a different bio-med doctor when Cameron was about eight. She insisted on seeing his little brother as well, and we make twice-yearly trips to Sydney to meet with her. She has been a godsend. All the things that the first bio-med doctor said are the things she says too, but it was all too much for me to cope with when Cameron was so little. We focus on getting diet right, improving gut health and getting zinc levels up and copper levels down, amongst other things. Cameron has learned to cope with blood tests. He became adept at swallowing pills when he was nine and now takes a daily cocktail of supplements, which have done him the world of good. He has also done Samonas Sound Therapy for auditory processing issues.

Personally, I have grown and changed plenty in seven years. I'm more relaxed. I'm no longer overcome by grief like I was. And my anxieties about Cameron's future have mostly been whittled away, little by little. A lot of that comes from simply looking back. I think about how I never thought he would manage at school - and yet, now he's at high school, doing fine. I think about how I wondered if he would ever speak in sentences - and yet, he can put any sentence together that he cares to (this is both good and bad...) I used to worry that he'd still be obsessing about Thomas when he was a teenager, but I can tell you, he's not. And even if he was, we'd be able to talk about it together and discuss it.

Meltdowns and difficulties have become a learning opportunity for us. Once things are calm, we are usually able to talk with him about what went wrong, and why, and how we might work together to do better next time. Every time Cameron overcomes a fear, tries something new or takes a tiny step towards competence, he is developing confidence and flexibility. As that grows, everything becomes easier, and it's fantastic, years later, to see good results emerging from all of those tiny steps.

I don't know what Cameron will do as a young adult and as he grows older. Most of the time, I'm actually not *that* worried about it. I've never been able to see more than about a year ahead with this kid, but things have worked out. What I've learned is that we just need to stay the course and take the constant, small steps that we need to take *today*. Yes, sure, they might be tiring steps, and annoying steps, and sometimes very difficult steps, but if we take them, they pay off for us.

At a difficult point in Year 7, I took Cameron to a child psychologist, just to see if she had anything to add. By the end of our session (I had been asked to stay in the room) she said, "I think you two are a bit of a team, aren't you?" and Cameron nodded. He knows that I and his dad will work things out with him, that we have his best interests at heart, and that we'll help him find solutions. We're on his side.

I kept writing my autism blog until Cameron was 12. After that, it seemed a little bit like a breach of privacy for a growing teenager so I stopped. The blog is still available online however. Just go to www.cecilypaterson.com/autism and check it out. I still love to hear from people who are beginning or part-way along their autism journey, so do get in touch if you want to.

I'm grateful to our various therapists and doctors, including our RDI (Relationship Development Intervention) consultant from years ago who gave us a marvellous foundation of how to develop relationship skills and how to help Cameron feel both competent and confident. We have used our scaffolding and calming skills in so many other areas of life. I think all parents (no, all people) should go and do RDI training.

I'm grateful to our 'village', the community in which we've lived for all of Cameron's school life thus far. Not only did the school support Cameron, but our church family also gave him all the time and space he needed, and our small town has been gracious, kind and generous to this kid who needed a bit of extra support. He even has a half hour 'job' in a local shop on Saturday afternoons, an amazing opportunity that would be a lot harder to find in a bigger community.

Also, I'm grateful for our wonderful doctor who has worked on Bright Eyes' biochemistry and found ways to help his body cope better with the day to day demands on him.

People say I don't acknowledge our own contribution, but believe me, I'm very aware of how hard both I and my husband have worked - and continue to work - to give our son a safe and stable platform from which he can launch into life.

We aren't there yet, of course, wherever 'there' is, but every day, you keep living life, and Cameron's a darn sight further along the road than he ever was. He's a smart, funny, thoughtful, insightful individual who has talents and dreams, and I think he'll go a long way towards achieving them.

This summary of seven years sounds a little bit like everything's been sunshine and roses (apart from the axe murdering, obviously). I want to say, it hasn't. There have been times in the last seven years that I've wanted to tear my hair out, or when I simply just didn't know what on earth to do next. But what's also true is that there has been a lot *more* sunshine, and quite a few good-smelling roses. And I'm sure that there will be more to come, alongside the meltdowns and the opportunities for the growth, and the simple *love* that we have for this incredible kid.

* * *

My standard advice for parents with newly-diagnosed ASD children

If you're a parent of child with autism, just starting out, here are the things I think you could do. They've made a huge difference for us. We continue to go down these roads and I'm also always looking for new things that might help.

1. *Investigate diet change and biochemistry issues. You can get a headstart by going to www.mindd.org if you're in Australia.*
2. *Investigate auditory processing disorder and sensory processing disorder.*
3. *Get into the Relationship Development Intervention program and work with a consultant. Yes, it's expensive. It's all expensive. It's worth it because you'll get results.*
4. *Dogs are very calming and promote greater levels of oxytocin (which equals love and relaxation) just from hanging out with them. If you can, get a really affectionate and sensible dog. It doesn't necessarily have to be trained as a therapy dog. Our dog is a King Charles Cavalier spaniel with a beautiful, calm temperament. She's worth her cost in dog food and vets fees.*
5. *If your child isn't sleeping, investigate liquid melatonin. It's available on the pharmacy shelf in the US and by prescription in Australia (or you can buy it online and bring it in.)*
6. *Love your kid. Pray for them. Spend time with them. Enjoy their strengths and support them in their weaknesses.*
7. *Also, love yourself. Get support for yourself and respite where needed. You're not super-parent of the year (well, you probably are, but you can't be that all the time). We're all human and we all need replenishment and someone to listen to us.*

8. *Do the work. Seriously, none of this is easy and all of it takes sustained, consistent determination. But you **can** do it - mostly because if you don't, no one else will. And you want your child to have the best quality of life possible.*
9. *Gather a group of people who'll support you, cheer you on, love your kid and pray for you. As they say, it takes a village, and if you don't live in one, you need to create one.*

Appendix: The Relationship Development Intervention program

What is RDI?

I've always struggled with how to explain RDI to the people who ask about it. I muddle around and feel like I'm losing myself in technical words. So it was great to hear the founder of the program, Dr Steven Gutstein, describe RDI simply as 'un-therapy'.

If we understand 'therapy' to be something extra or special or unusual, RDI is not therapy. It's just providing the opportunity for a child to relearn normal child development.

The only difference is that we have to slow it down, break it down and do it in a quieter, more deliberate way. It's a second chance to do what everyone else does—grow and develop those relationship connections in the brain.

It doesn't teach discrete skills. It doesn't provide rewards for behaviour. It doesn't follow the child's lead.

It aims to build new pathways in the brain. It aims to teach the thinking skills required in our crazy, messy world. The pathways and the thinking skills are the same ones that most other children pick up and learn without even trying. RDI is not re-inventing the wheel and teaching something new.

What does it treat?

The RDI program distinguishes between the 'core deficits' of autism, and what it calls 'co-occurring conditions'. The core deficits of autism include:

Emotional referencing

A person with ASD may be able to recognize and label emotions, but they won't necessarily check by looking at someone's face to see what they think or know to read someone's face to see what they are feeling.

Social co-regulation

Think of this as a social dance. People with ASD can follow a procedure and a script, but have trouble with the give and take of a regular, unpredictable conversation.

Declarative communication

People with ASD will use language as a means to an end. It's easy for them to say (if they have language), "I want a drink please." But they have a harder time sharing their experiences, saying something like, "I love orange juice much more than water."

Relative thinking

People with ASD can cope with things that are concrete and black and white. They love numbers and quantifiable things. But they have trouble with things that are dependent on variables or the situation at hand. Which is better, honey or peanut butter? Is Dad very cross, or only a little bit annoyed?

Flexible thinking

They can understand rules and procedures, but being flexible is difficult for them. If you normally go to the toilet at preschool after morning tea, can you cope if you're taken before morning tea? What about if you walk a different way to the shops? Or if the room looks different because Mum's moved the furniture around?

Past/future thinking

Most people have the ability to reflect on their past experiences, analyse them and use them to help make decisions for the future. People with ASD lack this and are often at a loss in their decision making.

Unfortunately, people who lack all these skills find it extremely difficult to live, work and relate in the real world. Life doesn't follow a simple script. It's messy, tricky and unpredictable. People who can't adjust are at a serious disadvantage.

Dr Gutstein says, "Data shows that of adults with autism with normal IQ and language, only 3 per cent can live normally. That's because we're not treating autism itself.[1]"

Other things that show up

Co-occurring conditions are things that are sometimes associated with autism. For example, the gut and digestion and diet issues, or the sensory challenges that so many cope with. Then there are epileptic fits or self-stimulating (stimming) behaviours like hand-flapping, toe-walking or rocking, to name a few. Such conditions may occur in people without autism.

RDI doesn't treat these, but recommends that if they are becoming a 'block' to continuing progress, they should be looked at. For example, our consultant suggested that we look into Cameron's diet, as he exhibited unusual eating, toileting and skin patterns.

For us, the diet and biomedical treatments are helping get Cameron's brain into the optimal shape possible to learn, through RDI, the things he has not been able to learn yet because of the autism.

So how does it all work?

RDI takes practically every piece of research on child development ever written and breaks it down into 'objectives'. The objectives are then ordered into developmental 'stages'. Anyone who starts the RDI program, no matter if they are 3 or 30, starts at the beginning and masters the early objectives of understanding autism and a commitment to change before moving on to the developmental ones.

The logic is simple. In real life, a baby learns early on to follow a face and connect that face to a voice. As time goes on, she learns to give some sort of response. But if she's never mastered those skills, we can't expect her to be able to play peek-a-boo successfully when she's six months old. And if she has never mastered peek-a-boo, how can we expect her to be able to know how to play hide and seek with two friends when she's three or a game of sardines with a whole birthday party full of children at ten?

To be successful in relationships, every child needs to master the baby, toddler and preschooler basics first. So RDI children start back at the beginning and create the early connections they missed out on in their first years.

But all this work is not done with outside specialist therapists. RDI is primarily a parent and family-based program, with parents being 'coached' by the RDI consultant. This is because typical early child development occurs in the context of the parent-child relationship, or as researchers put it, the 'guided-participation relationship'.

Children first learn to engage with others through play and activities with their parents when they are babies and toddlers. As they grow and become more competent in different skills and tasks, they are also learning emotional referencing, relative thinking, flexibility and all the things that help real people live real lives in the real world.

It's as much for parents as for kids

The RDI program helps parents learn as much as their children in how to slow down, how to engage their child and how to begin to rebuild the relationship that will be the foundation for their child's growth.

Dr Gutstein described it like this:

"Rather than engaging in repetitive, rote-memory exercises typical of behavioural interventions, children in the RDI program rake leaves, prune trees, buy groceries, fix car engines and otherwise share the simple joys of everyday experiences with their parents… We focus on fostering loving relationships to enhance quality of life, rather than on behaviour modification aimed at teaching children on the autism spectrum to perform scripted behaviours."

Practically, that means spending at least half an hour a day, working with your child in specifically focused ways, helping them grasp and then master the developmental objectives. Many more hours are spent with less focus, but equal importance 'on the fly'. Outcomes are better if family life in general is more deliberate and more thoughtful, and if the TV and computer stay off! As with any child, the more productive time you put in, the greater the likelihood is of a better outcome.

More than just early intervention

And for anyone who thinks that RDI is only for little children and couldn't possibly help a teenager or even an adult, there's hope.

Gutstein argues that, "while many characteristics of ASD seem to improve with time and/or instruction, the conventional wisdom has been that experience-sharing deficits are lifelong and resistant to treatment. We reject that notion."

It's a program for children, teens and adults alike and it does not accept that once you reach a certain age, all brain development is finished.

Is RDI for you?

Read more about RDI: https://www.rdiconnect.com/

Get started with RDI in Australia: http://rdiconsultantsaustralia.com.au/

[1] Quoted in the article *Ped Med: Autism therapies vary*, March 19 2007, published by United Press International at www.upi.com

Extra resources

Books

***Autism Aspergers: Solving the Relationship Puzzle—A New Developmental Program that Opens the Door to Lifelong Social and Emotional Growth*, Steven E. Gutstein, 2001, Future Horizons**
This book has lots of practical things you can do at home with your child.

***Gut and Psychology Syndrome*, Dr. Natasha Cameron-McBride, 2004 Medinform Publishing**
A wonderfully clear explanation of the effect of the gut and digestion on the brain, and some ideas on how to get a child to eat good foods. (Hey, although they didn't work for me, it doesn't mean they're no good!)

***I Love you Rituals*, Dr Rebecca Anne Bailey, 2000, Harper paperbacks**
A lovely book with wonderful ideas on how to spend quality time with all your children.

***Learning as we Grow*, Beurkens, Roon & Kowalczyk, published by Horizons centre, available online at http://www.horizonsdrc.com/store/learning-as-we-grow

This book is great for practical ideas to make school life easier for child and teacher.

My Baby Can Dance: Stories of Autism, Asperger's and Success Through the Relationship Development Intervention (RDI) Program, **Steven E. Gutstein (ed), 2006, Connections Center Publications**

Some real life stories of families doing the RDI program.

Raising Our Children, Raising Ourselves: Transforming parent-child relationships from reaction and struggle to freedom, power and joy, **Naomi Aldort, 2005, Book Publishers Network**

This book was instrumental in me becoming a much more 'free' and accepting parent. Even if you don't love every part of it, it's worth a read, just to stretch your horizons.

Take heart—For families living with disability, **Kate Hurley (ed), 2009** ***Blue Bottle Press***

Thoughts on God, the bible, disability and the gifts and tragedies that can go hand in hand.

The Brain That Changes Itself: Stories of personal triumph from the frontiers of brain science, **Norman Doidge, MD, 2010, Scribe Publications**

These stories gave me hope that learning and retraining the brain was possible at any age. The pressure of 'early intervention' above everything, and not 'running out of time' was abated somewhat when I read it.

***The Explosive Child: A New Approach for Understanding and Parenting Easily Frustrated, Chronically Inflexible Children*, Ross W Greene, 2010, Harper Paperbacks**
Practical, paradigm-changing and worth every cent. I love this book and I keep giving it away because *everyone* needs a copy.

***The RDI Book: Forging New Pathways for Autism, Aspergers and PDD with the Relationship Development Intervention Program*, Gutstein, Baird & Gutstein, 2009, Connections Center**
Probably the most comprehensive explanation of the basic concepts of the RDI program and the science behind them. It's not an easy read, but very worthwhile.

***The Whole-Brain Child: Revolutionary Strategies to Nurture Your Child's Developing Mind*, Daniel J Siegel MD, Tina Payne Bryson PhD, 2011, Delacorte Press, New York**
A very practical, wonderful book for all families. It has some great cartoons you can use to help explain things to children.

***The Woman Who Changed Her Brain: Unlocking the Extraordinary Potential of the Human Mind*, Barbara Arrowsmith-Young, 2012, Square Peg**
This was a great story, which made me ask lots of questions about what might be possible. I'm waiting for her school to start up in Australia!

***Understanding Pathological Demand Avoidance Syndrom in Children: A Guide for Parents, Teachers and Other Professionals*, Phil Christie, Margaret Duncan, Ruth Fidler and Zara Healey, 2012, Jessica Kingsley Publishers, London**

I investigated this long-sounding title because it seemed so relevant to Cameron, who would avoid and resist anything and everything for a very long time. There were useful parts, and I recommend it to parents whose children are chronic refusers.

Websites

www.amaze.org.au

If lobbying government and working for change interests you, you could get involved here

www.autismspectrum.org.au

This is a place to start if you're looking for a diagnosis or some immediate help or resources or to sort out early intervention government funding.

auwww.braingym.org.

Cameron benefited from kinesiology in the year that he started school. It helped his coordination, concentration and fine motor skills.

www.cecilypaterson.com/autism

I wrote about Cameron's journey here in detail up until he was 12, when I stopped for the sake of his privacy. Teenagers, you know? You can still access the blog posts, however, and I'm always happy to connect with parents who want to chat more. Use my 'Contact' form on the website.

www.connectandrelateforautism.com.au

www.rdiconsultantsaustralia.com.au

Look at these two sites here to find an RDI consultant in Australia.

www.familyconnections.com.au

We were impressed with the care and expertise of this group when Cameron attended a school-age social skills program when he was about 10.

www.learningdiscoveries.com.au

An Aussie holistic therapy provider with lots of useful approaches. If you're interested in reading about Samonas Sound Therapy for auditory processing disorder this would be a good start.

www.livesinthebalance.org

If you liked the sound of Dr Greene's three basket approach, check out his website here.

www.karunahealthcare.com.au

Homeopathy has definitely helped Cameron's moods and outlook on life and is worth a try.

www.horizonsdrc.com

This is a US based site. I like the way it takes a holistic approach to the issues. It has a good blog to follow and plenty of practical information.

www.au.iherb.com

We get a lot of our supplements from this site which has great prices and fast shipping. They have liquid melatonin, and they are also the only place I have ever found the slow release 100mg zinc tablets that have been so helpful to Cameron. (They are prescribed by our doctor, along with a swathe of other vitamins and oils.)

www.jacobs-journey.blogspot.com

This blog by a mum of a young boy with ASD inspired me to continue on and to work to see the same amazing results for my son. She hasn't written in it for a while, but it's still a good resource to look back on.

www.mindd.org

All about nutrition and its effect on the brain—not just concerning ASD, but also diabetes, asthma, ADHD, dyspraxia and dyslexia. There are good resources to be found here and details about conferences and seminars in Australia. I think this site is most useful for its list of Australian doctors and allied health professionals who tread a similar path to our wonder-working GP.

www.rdiconnect.com

The home page of the Relationship Development Intervention program. Lots here—including forums and information.

Acknowledgements

Many people read the manuscript and offered help, editing, suggestions and support, including Liz, Sarah, Rebekah, Katrina, Linda, Rena and Karen. Kate Hurley fielded a number of phone calls and emails and kept me believing that I needed to put the book out there. Of course, a big thank you to my husband Andrew who always encourages me to write and loudly supports whatever I do.

I was delighted that *Love Tears & Autism* won third prize in the Australian Christian Book of the Year Awards in 2012, despite my pathetic and teary attempt at a thank you speech on the night. Thanks go to the ACBOY organisers for their support, and for the support of so many wonderful readers who embraced this story with open hearts. My story is your story too.

A personal request from the author

If you found this book helpful, I'd really appreciate it if you'd leave an online review, either where you purchased it, on Goodreads, or on social media. And if you're reading a paperback copy, consider buying another to give to your local preschool, creche or kindergarten for their resources shelf. This independent author will thank *you* for your support.

Connect with Cecily Paterson

On the net, www.cecilypaterson.com is my regular website. My blog about Cameron is found at www.cecilypaterson.com/autism. It includes details of our life, therapy and adventures together up until he turned twelve. You can write to me through the contact form on the website. I love to hear from readers, and I will always answer your messages. Alternatively, find me on Facebook, Twitter and Instagram @CecilyPaterson.

Also by Cecily Paterson

In the seven years since *Love Tears & Autism* was published, I have done more writing, of what I call 'brave-hearted' fiction for girls, creating 'stories that stay with you, and characters that become friends'. My novels are realistic fiction and best suit girls aged 10-14. Find my books online under the name of Cecily Anne Paterson, or on my website at www.cecilypaterson.com

And there's more: I publish Christian colouring books at www.firewheelpress.com

Want to write your memoir? I'll teach you how at www.red-loungeforwriters.com

www.ingramcontent.com/pod-product-compliance
Lightning Source LLC
Chambersburg PA
CBHW030436010526
44118CB00011B/658